# A LIFE IN PIECES

# A
# Life
# in
# Pieces

Jo-Ann Wallace

Thistledown Press

Thistledown Press Ltd.
Unit 222, 220 20TH Street w
Saskatoon, SK  S7M 0W9
www.thistledownpress.com

Library and Archives Canada Cataloguing in Publication

Title: A life in pieces / by Jo-Ann Wallace.
Names: Wallace, Jo-Ann, 1953- author.
Identifiers: Canadiana (print) 20240364082 | Canadiana (ebook) 20240364228 | ISBN 9781771872560 (softcover) | ISBN 9781771872652 (EPUB)
Subjects: LCSH: Wallace, Jo-Ann, 1953- | LCSH: College teachers—Canada—Biography. | CSH: Authors, Canadian (English)—21st century—Biography. | LCGFT: Autobiographies.
Classification: LCC PS8645.A467375 Z46 2024 | DDC C818/.603—dc23

Edited by Susan Olding
Cover and book design by Betsy Rosenwald
Cover image: Russel Wright residential melmac cups
Printed and bound in Canada

Thistledown Press gratefully acknowledges the financial assistance of SK Arts, The Canada Council for the Arts, and the Government of Canada for its publishing program.

*For Stephen*

I had a flashback of something that never existed.

Louise Bourgeois

# CONTENTS

# Memoir of the Lives I Didn't Live

FOR MY ENTIRE ADULT LIFE, I HAVE BEEN HAUNTED by the idea that there is—somewhere out there, maybe in another city, maybe in this city—another me. My doppelgänger goes about her day, living the life I was intended to live but that I somehow escaped. She lives in a two-bedroom walk-up apartment building, grateful that she has a balcony and a view of the park. She takes the bus, and, in my mind's eye, that is where I often see her, sitting and watching the passing streetscape. I also see her at the grocery store, pushing her cart and adding up, in her mind, the cost of the items she has placed there. She always pays with cash and has to make sure she has enough in her wallet. Sometimes I see her at the Army & Navy, holding up small items of clothing, assessing their suitability. Everything she buys has to serve multiple functions. What these other functions are, I don't know because when I see her, she is always alone. But she is not lonely. I used to see her pushing a stroller down the street and that is clearly why she lives the life she does. She is a single mother. Somehow, she has not kept pace with my aging. She is no longer young, but neither is she old. All the walking and all the watching of pennies have kept her slim, but she passes invisibly on the street and not only because she is a doppelgänger. She is just one of those people.

Is she happy? That is a question I have never been able to answer because happiness seems beside the point. Is she satisfied? That is a more pertinent question. Even more pertinent: is she less or more satisfied than I am? I have had a career; I live in a house, and I retreat to a second home in the mountains; I have a congenial husband and a little dog. I would like to think that she also has a small totem animal to keep her company, but it's difficult to find rental apartments that permit them. At the same time, her satisfactions are real and mostly the same as mine. She loves to watch the trees waving their arms in the air—making the wind, as she thought when she was little. She finds shadows inexplicably moving. She observes the seasons and small dramas on the street. She eavesdrops in public places, especially on the bus and in the city library. Now and then she treats herself to a McChicken burger at McDonald's and she eavesdrops there too. Sometimes she wonders what her doppelgänger is up to and sometimes she wonders whose is the more satisfying life.

I leave her, my benign doppelgänger, gazing out the bus window and thinking she has just caught sight of me hurrying to my car with my briefcase stuffed full of books and lecture notes. (She romanticizes, just a little, my job.) But there is another, more hazily sketched, me out there, a me I hesitate to bring to consciousness. But sometimes I read about her in the newspapers and a hand squeezes my heart, hard. Her guilt overwhelms me, and I take on the shame she will not. I am like Virginia Woolf's Clarissa Dalloway who, on hearing of Septimus's suicide, must live it. "Always her body went through it, when she was told, first, suddenly, of an accident;

her dress flamed, her body burnt." In this case, though, it is not my doppelgänger's body that burns, that is impaled, drowned, broken, and what I experience is something more like complicity. The rush of anger, the you-little-bastard, the shut-the-fuck-up-just-for-once-shut-the-fuck-up. I lash out, there is a snap or a crack or sudden total silence and that's it. My heart thumps once but I bring down the veil, I shut that door, I'm not going there. Nobody ever thinks about me, about what I have to put up with, what it's like never having a minute to myself. Easy for them. Or maybe I am swallowed by despair, overwhelming, a room without doors or windows. There is nothing nothing nothing and my little ones, my little chickens, my kittens, cannot live without their mother who loves them better than anything. I take strawberry yoghurt, better for them than ice cream, and I put medicine in it. I take some medicine too and we all snuggle in my bed, under my down comforter. But I am the only one who wakes up, groggy in a small crusty pool of vomit. What have I done? But I shut that door. It's not my fault and anyway they belonged to me.

It occurs to me that I write about my benign doppelgänger, the one who goes about her modest life, in the third person while my Edward Hyde, the one who rises in my gorge, claims the first. This is not how Henry Jekyll feels when he writes his long confessional letter in the handwriting he shares with Hyde: "He, I say—I cannot say, I." The disavowed monster, the shrunken dwarf who lives in our blood, the furious Rumpelstiltskin who tears himself, and us, in two. Or rather, "herself" because my doppelgängers are always women, and their experiences are always the experiences of women and of women's bodies.

But what is the opposite of a doppelgänger, the antithesis of me? Because I've run into them, too. In my mind I call them The Tidy Girls and my encounters with them have always been fleeting but weirdly memorable. The first was Pat. I was eight years old, maybe nine, and I was at a Brownies meeting, though I don't know how this was possible because I don't remember having a Brownies uniform until I was a year or two older, and, even then, it was second-hand and a little faded. Anyway, there we were, sitting in a circle, and Brown Owl was talking about the importance of clean nails. We all had to hold our hands out so that our nails could be inspected and commented upon. Mine, as always, were a mess, but Pat had beautiful nails, clean, the cuticles pushed right down, small white crescent moons of nail extending over the ends of her little girl fingers. And a quiet demure face with tidy hair. I felt a kind of awe but without envy, because even then I knew this was an apotheosis of femininity that I could never attain. And then, years later, I am on an old repurposed yellow school bus rattling through suburban streets, on my way to the latest in a series of ridiculous jobs I held after quitting school. Sitting on the seat opposite me is a slim girl, about my age, eighteen or nineteen, straight brunette hair in a tidy bob, the kind of brunette with pale freckled skin. The bus has no suspension, and we are tossed painfully up and down, but she sits very still with her hands resting palm up on the seat beside her. Palm up. Why does this make such an impression on me? Is it because it represents a kind of patient receptivity, a calm empty waiting? Later I try to emulate this posture, my hands on either side of me, resting palm up, but let's face it, I can't carry it off. Fast-forward three or four years and I am back at school, in the university library and ravenous for the life of the mind. I go to the stacks for a book and, as I return to my seat, a girl passes me wafting a faint perfume. She is blonde and tidy, a good girl and a little unimaginative,

I think, not the kind of person that I would want to be friends with. And yet I go a little weak in the knees, something about the perfume, about that soft modesty, that impenetrable Madonna-like femininity. I am a good enough girl to desire it, to want to be it, but I am also a smart enough girl to want something else, something bigger and messier, something more like Simone de Beauvoir or Gwendolyn MacEwen or even, in my wilder imaginings, Janis Joplin.

And of course, I am none of these. Neither good girl nor bad girl. I think again of Clarissa Dalloway who imagines herself carrying her life in her arms, showing it to her long dead parents and saying "This is what I have made of it! This!" And then she wonders, "And what had she made of it? What, indeed?"

# EARLY

# 43 Leslie Gault

I'VE JUST FINISHED READING A 2003 MEMOIR BY Hilary Mantel. In it she writes this: "All your houses are haunted by the person you might have been." The sentence struck me with some force because I have been thinking about time travel, about the desire to travel back to other times and places. My own places, my own houses and apartments, but other places too. Sometimes I go to Google street maps and take a virtual walk past the places in which I used to live. They are changed but not beyond recognition.

Here is 43 Leslie Gault, in the neighbourhood of Ahuntsic, in the city of Montreal. I lived here from the time I was three until I was almost ten. From the outside, the building—a fourplex—is unchanged. There is the driveway sloping steeply down to the garage. When I was four or five I watched some big boys ride their two-wheel bicycles down that slope, pedalling backwards to break hard just before they reached the garage door. Down I went on my tricycle, pedalling backwards to no avail. I'm sure my wails could be heard across the neighbourhood.

Walk in the outside door of number 43, past the inside front door of the Bergerons, our landlords, and go up the staircase to our apartment. It is the staircase on which I sat as I translated conversations between Madame Bergeron and my mother. Groceries, baby carriages, tricycles, and sleds went up and down those stairs. Open the front door onto the hallway that runs the length of the apartment. Turn left and then left again and you are in the kitchen. It is not large but my parents managed to cram fifteen adults and children in there for Christmas dinner, a dinner punctuated by rye and ginger ale, canned cranberry jelly, and unaccustomed pickles. Little pink planters from Occupied Japan with stylized black cats lived on the kitchen walls, small tendrils of something trailing out. The wringer washing machine also lived in the kitchen though I can't quite remember where. It must have been beside the door to the back balcony. The spiral iron staircase to the backyard took me past the next-door boxer dog, leaping up against the fence and barking in a terrifying way. I sometimes shimmied down the central iron post rather than risk an encounter. The backyard was unadorned, the lawn untended, though occasionally Louise Bergeron's little wading pool would appear, and I would be invited to join. Once a neighbourhood boy peed against the wall, drawing a circle, a performance that impressed me enormously and made me wish for a penis. For a while I pretended I had a penis.

I think about what 43 Leslie Gault would have smelled like. In those years—in fact, for much of the twentieth century—we lived in a deep fug of cigarette smoke. My parents were both heavy smokers and our apartment had to be painted every two or three years to hide the yellow tar that gathered high up on the walls. When we took the bus or the streetcar we were wedged in with people smoking, inadvertently burning holes in each other's clothing. Holes in clothing, holes in upholstery, burn marks on coffee tables. And ashtrays. Murano glass ashtrays; ashtrays that were pieces of furniture, perched on their own pedestals; boomerang-shaped ceramic ashtrays; Spin-o-Matic self-cleaning ashtrays; primitive clay ashtrays that kids made at school for Father's Day.

Of course, 43 Leslie Gault had other smells too, breakthrough smells. Pot roast on Sundays. The smell of laundry making its squelchy way through the wringer washer. The smell of sheets frozen solid as my mother brought them in from the clothesline in winter. The hot smell of early summer, the kitchen door to the balcony wide open, the radio tuned to CJAD, maple whirligigs drifting in the wind and gathering in small mounds on the ground. The smell of my father's aftershave. The inevitable smells of vomit and fever and calamine lotion in a small apartment with four tiny children.

Across the hall from the kitchen is Catherine and Laura's bedroom where the toybox lives. Next to that is the bedroom I share with Nancy. Lying in bed, weeping helplessly in the wake of some slight or reprimand from my parents. Snot clogging my airways. "I can't breathe," I sob. Nancy, in a panic in her neighbouring bed, calls out to our parents. "Jo-Ann can't breathe." They are unrepentant in the living room, their bums planted firmly on the slippery loopy fabric of the chesterfield. The chesterfield leaves a pattern on your face if you fall asleep on it. Also in the living room is the new television set which gives us Bonanza and Walt Disney. If I put my head in my mother's lap while we watch TV, she will strokingly tuck my hair behind my ear.

Opposite the living room, at the far end of the long hallway, is my parents' bedroom. Dark, heavy second-hand furniture. A closet that is good to hide in, their clothes brushing my face. A vanity with mirrors that fold in on themselves so I am multiplied infinitely. On and on I go. I feel sure there is a way to step into this world of many me's. I just have to find the key. In the meantime, I put on plays in this room, forcing my parents to sit on the bed and watch as my sisters and I skate around on the waxed and polished wooden floor. Sometimes I wear a crinoline on my head. Long golden hair. Sometimes I wake in the middle of the night and make my way to their bedroom, where I curl up like a puppy on the small carpet at the foot of their bed.

That is our indoor life. Sometimes Madame Bergeron, who has only three children and a piano, gets cross at the sound of eight small feet running up and down the long hallway. My mother gets cross at Madame Bergeron. My parents scrape together the money and we move to a brand new, split level house in the suburbs. The house is perhaps 1200 square feet and my mother worries how she will ever keep such a large house clean.

Who, to go back to Hilary Mantel, is the person I might have been in that apartment? Who is the me who haunts it? I find it so difficult to answer that question. I can only imagine a skinny-legged seven-year-old, exploring a world circumscribed by a couple of city blocks. Trying to match what she was reading to what she was seeing. Wanting a dog more than almost anything. But that is not the kind of answer Hilary Mantel is looking for. She means "the ghosts of other lives you might have led." My imagination doesn't go there. I can only imagine my subsequent houses and my subsequent lives. I can only imagine the finality of me, all roads leading here.

For many years I had a recurring dream which, sadly, has abandoned me in the last couple of years. I miss it. There were a couple of versions but the basic theme remained the same.

I am in a house and suddenly I discover a secret room that I didn't know was there. My house opens onto a whole new space. In one version, it's a series of rooms, bedrooms I think. Now that I think of it, the bedrooms are linked by a long hallway. In the more usual version, a massive space at the top of the house suddenly presents itself. It is a kind of attic, large, and, in its vastness and its bridge-like structures, much like Piranesi's fantastical prison etchings. It's not a particularly happy place. There is something almost dreary about it. But I desire it greatly. I love the sudden expansion and the sense of a secret place. Who am I in that space? Who is the me who produces such a space?

I want that dream back.

# Two Books

*They lived in houses in which books were part of existence and the intellect was prized.*

Noel Annan, "The Intellectual Aristocracy"

OURS WAS NOT A HOUSE IN WHICH BOOKS WERE a necessary part of existence, nor was it a house that prized the intellect. In the upper fourplex of my early years there were newspapers and sometimes colouring books; there were, briefly, several of the Best in Children's Books, a Nelson Doubleday series that my parents subscribed to in the very late 1950s. There were cereal boxes, a last resort when all other reading materials had been exhausted. There was a radio that played all day—"Que Sera Sera," "Love and Marriage"—and eventually there was a television set. But our household held only two proper, grown-up books, by which I mean books with chapters and only a few pictures. In those years my parents did not own books and they did not borrow books.

It was not until we moved to one of the new suburban developments that were sprouting like mushrooms across Montreal's West Island that we joined a public library. I was almost ten years old. The library comprised two rooms of an old bungalow, a remnant of our shiny new suburb's former village life. It smelled tantalizingly of damp wood and ancient carpets, and it held more books than I had ever seen in one place.

Among them was a biography of Maurice "Rocket" Richard that I swallowed in one gulp, compelled by the story of the riot that erupted along St. Catherine Street in March 1955 when NHL president Clarence Campbell suspended the Rocket for the remainder of the season and the playoffs. It was so unfair! The suspension deprived the Rocket of the scoring title for that year, and it deprived the Canadiens of the Stanley Cup. Twenty thousand fans smashed windows and doors and looted businesses.

While Montreal was rioting, Noel Annan was publishing his article on the intellectual aristocracy—the English intellectual aristocracy, it goes without saying. The *Oxford English Dictionary* grudgingly and parsimoniously defines "the intellect" as "analytic intelligence," and Annan is only a little more forthcoming. His "intellectual aristocracy"—the generations of English men and women that, among other accomplishments, gave rise to the great flowering of the Bloomsbury Group—is defined as much by absences as by qualities: they were families who despised "polished manners" and "the art of pleasing"; they had little feeling for the fine arts although "literature was in their bones"; they were "ascetic," utilitarian, committed to distinguishing the "sham from the genuine, appearance from reality."

They were *nothing* like my family.

My family's ethos (Annan's word—certainly not ours) was determined largely by my mother and her two sisters. Theirs was a decidedly female ethos, woven on the streets of

Park Extension and Mile End and Lachine. The spider web of attachment that Virginia Woolf describes in *Mrs. Dalloway*—the "thin thread" of affection that "stretch[es] and stretch[es]," gets "thinner and thinner" until, "burdened," it "sags down"—never had to stretch farther than a streetcar ride. It was a network of aunts and sisters and cousins and great aunts and honorary aunts.

They valued laughter, gossip, and talk. Endless talk, during visits, on the telephone, in the kitchen while ironing. Which is where, at a young age, I learned from my mother that Rock Hudson was gay and Bobby Darin had a heart condition. In the absence of sisters, it was permissible to gossip with your children. Talk was valued, words were a kind of currency, but a currency with all the weight of helium. Words were there to interweave and to connect, but also to fill space up and to deflect. The intellect, had they ever thought in those terms, was held in great suspicion as a kind of foreign affectation, like baguettes or berets.

But what of my father's family, who were altogether weightier and a little more mysterious, though no more invested in the "intellect"? Immigrants from the Scottish Lowlands where they worked in the shale mines, they seemed to span a wilder and more serious gamut, from fraudsters, bookies and adulteresses to Pentecostal ministers. They did not send words out into the world like balloons; they harboured them and heaved them like rocks.

My father's mother's maiden name, astonishingly, was Bookless. This has never been a common name and its meaning has been a source of some debate. In 1858, Robert Ferguson, in his dictionary of British surnames, suggested, a bit hopefully, that the name derived from the Norse bokloes or book-learned: "Not so called from the scantiness of his library, but rather from the good use he made of what he had." An 1864 reviewer remarked, tartly, that if the name Legless appears in the fourteenth or fifteenth century or later, "we can only suppose it means what it appears to mean, and that it is a sobriquet given to a man who had lost one or both of his legs. Even in Saxon times," the reviewer continued, relentlessly, "it is hard to believe that Witless, the father of Wambs, was distinguished for his wisdom." The great Bookless debate was obviously a thing of the moment and, by 1882, Abram Smythe Palmer's *Folk Etymology* concluded that Bookless is of Gaelic origin and likely means "yellow water," something of a scatological come down.

Nonetheless, and in spite of the fact that a good percentage of our genetic makeup is Bookless, there were two books in our upper fourplex and between the ages of seven and ten I read them and reread them and puzzled over them. They were: *Mary Poppins Comes Back* by P. L. Travers and *Belles on Their Toes* by Frank Gilbreth, Jr. and Ernestine Gilbreth Carey. How these two books made their way to our home, I have no idea. Could they have been wedding presents to my parents? Or maybe they arrived stuffed in a box of hand-me-downs for a young couple just starting out, crammed in with the used pots and pans and second-hand Christmas ornaments. Regardless of how they got there, there they were. They were books, the only ones we had and the first ones I knew.

First, but not first. Both books are sequels. The real story, the inauguration story, the creation myth is elsewhere, off stage. Mary Poppins—in some other world, in some other book—has already made her way to Cherry Tree Lane, made herself indispensable, and flown away under her umbrella, and now she returns. Other people, other readers, already know all about her. I am late to the party. *Belles on Their Toes* is the sequel to *Cheaper by the Dozen*, the story of Frank and Lillian Gilbreth, pioneering time-motion study and efficiency experts, and their twelve children. *Belles on Their Toes*, the sequel, opens under the cloud of Frank's death as his widow attempts to run their business and raise their family, alone.

What did I want from books in those very early days? Pretty much the same thing I want from them now. I wanted to know how to live—that is, what to expect—and I wanted something like magic, which is the thing that makes the world bigger. It is the wardrobe that opens onto Narnia but it is also Ethiopians making coffee in Camilla Gibb's *Sweetness in the Belly*: roasting green coffee beans over a hibachi in Harari or a Bunsen burner in London, grinding the roasted beans together with a cardamom pod, and serving the thick coffee in tiny cups.

P. L. Travers's Mary Poppins is no Disneyfied "spoonful of sugar" nanny. She does not make anything bigger. She is vain. She snaps, pushes, glares "with angry eyes," speaks "acidly" or "tartly," and she lies. Her magic is punitive and confining: trapping Mr. Banks's nasty old governess in a bird-cage, sequestering Jane in the world of the Royal Doulton bowl. Truth be told, Mary Poppins—with her throat lozenges, seven flannel nightgowns, and four cotton ones—reminded me of the nuns we still saw everywhere in pre-Vatican II Montreal, in their long black habits and their angry withholding faces.

*Belles on Their Toes* was a very different kettle of fish. In some ways it was completely bewildering. The Gilbreth family, we are told repeatedly, is poor, and yet they have a man-of-all-work—the stage Irish Tom—to whom they condescend, and a big house, and they go to the seaside for the summer.

But... *but*... there was the magic, the romance of efficiency. In *Belles on Their Toes*, I got only the belated echo of the pioneering efficiency innovations of *Cheaper by the Dozen*, but it was enough to sharpen my imagination. Mr. Gilbreth has already organized his household "on an efficiency basis, just as he organized a factory." He has already instituted "the process charts" which told the children "what we were supposed to do and when we were supposed to do it." He has already assigned each of the children "a number, which he used for routing intra-family correspondence and memoranda." And, most fascinating of all, he had "made motion studies of himself, so he could sleep later in the mornings," "lather[ing] his face with two shaving brushes, to save time" and figuring out the most efficient way to wield a bar of soap so that he "could get into a tub, soap himself, rinse, and get out again, in a minute or less."

Why did this take such a hold of my imagination, so that even today I have to shake myself and make myself take unnecessary steps, make unnecessary movements? I think that, for the very blank slate that was my young mind, efficiency was a kind of poetry. And even now I think of poetry as a kind of efficiency, the most efficient, elegant *because* efficient, use of language.

My Bookless grandmother knew something about efficiency herself. She worked as a waitress in Eaton's famous ninth-floor art deco restaurant in Montreal. Now remembered as Le 9e, which certainly would not have been its name when my grandmother worked there, it was designed by French architect Jacques Carlu to resemble the dining hall of the *Île de France*, purportedly Lady Eaton's favourite ocean liner. The waitresses—for, unlike most high-end restaurants, the servers at Le 9e were all women—were trained to take orders, even from large groups, without writing anything down, their hands behind their backs. And they were trained never to go to or from the kitchen without carrying something, a habit my grandmother retained throughout her life.

In *Belles on Their Toes*, industrial engineer Lillian Gilbreth designs an "efficiency kitchen," where everything necessary to put a meal on the table—refrigerator, pantry, stove, sink—can be reached with a minimum of steps. This is such a novelty in 1924 that the local newspaper wants to photograph her baking a cake in her own kitchen. But Mrs. Gilbreth lives in a house whose kitchen was designed "to accommodate three or four servants," though she is now reduced to one. Some fancy footwork, while their man-of-all-work is away on his day off, temporarily transforms the Gilbreths' enormous kitchen into "an efficiency type kitchenette of the kind used today in a good many apartments." Photographs are taken. The fiction is preserved. But, of course, efficiency was not a choice or an ideal for working-class women like my Bookless grandmother. It was a condition of life.

# The Halfway Tavern

THE HALFWAY TAVERN—SO CALLED BECAUSE IT was on Park Avenue, halfway between St. Viateur and Fairmount—was for decades my maternal grandfather's watering hole. It was only a short city block from his home on Jeanne Mance and seemed, in my childhood, to be the stuff of legend. They all drank there, and by "all" I mean all the men in what was already a large extended family, one that continued to grow when my mother and her two sisters reached their dating and marrying years. Brothers, uncles, cousins, second cousins, in-laws, second cousins of in-laws. All men, because, until 1979, women were forbidden, by law, from setting foot in Montreal's taverns.

My own very early memories of the Halfway Tavern are benign, mostly of hot summer afternoons at my grandparents' apartment, the men disappearing for a couple of hours and returning to fall asleep in their chairs. But there were other stories, including one about a family brawl that took place outside the Halfway Tavern before I was born, my paternal Scottish grandfather goaded beyond bearing by my maternal aunt's fiancé. "Where's the rock, Jock?" my future uncle taunted. This led to some inevitable back and forth and then the farcical: a handful of men engaging in fisticuffs on the streets of Montreal because, an ocean away, a small group of students had stolen the Scottish Stone of Scone, the Stone of Destiny.

By the time I heard such stories, we had moved to our brand new West Island suburb, far from the inner-city taverns. My mother's mother had died a couple of years earlier and my mother began to put a little distance between herself and her father. It's hard to know exactly why, though, like many men of his time and class, Aubrey Cotton threw his weight around at home. As a child he had suffered from rickets, spending years on crutches, and as a result he was a small man. His attestation paper, when he signed up for the war in 1916, put his height at five feet two inches. In the British army this would have seen him placed in one of the newly formed Bantam units for men, mostly from the industrial and coalmining north, who were under five feet three inches. Whatever her reasons for turning her back on her father, my mother retained a strong distrust of short men and consequently married a tall one.

Aubrey's father, William, had worked as a groom in what my mother described as "a big house," somewhere in the Midlands, before he emigrated to a small town in southwestern Quebec with his wife and young children when Aubrey was eight. My mother recalls that William always touched his cap when he spoke to people and showed up every Saturday to help his daughter-in-law, my grandmother, with the heavy chores. Aubrey did not inherit his father's self-effacing ways. Nonetheless, as a young man he must have had a certain charm because he somehow attracted the convent-educated daughter of a white-collar family. Having attracted her, he set about not supporting her in the manner to which she was accustomed, instead scraping together a living from odd jobs as a handyman carpenter and caretaker of the block of flats in which they lived at the corner of Jeanne Mance and St. Viateur. The building was across the street from a small Jewish Orthodox synagogue and my mother earned a nickel there every Saturday morning for going in and turning on the lights before the Shabbat service.

Aubrey was a man of contradictions. His mother taught him to tat and crochet when he was in bed with rickets, and he later crocheted a boudoir cap for his young bride and lined it with silk. He inherited his skill as a carpenter from his mother's side of the family—her father, Aubrey's grandfather, was a coffin maker in Sunderland and she sewed the coffin linings. Aubrey had a temper, but he also loved children, entering my mother in a beautiful baby contest when she was a toddler. The professional photo portrait taken of her must have been an unusual luxury. When I was two he made me a little stool so that I could sit with the adults and take part in their conversation. I still have it and his penciled inscription underneath the seat—Jo-Ann's stool—is still visible. Every year he played Santa Claus at the carpenters' union Christmas party.

But Aubrey's love of children apparently waned over the years. He died when I was twenty-two and, to my delight, several of the now elderly denizens of the Halfway Tavern showed up for the funeral service and wake. They pulled us aside to share their stories about Aubrey, including how he liked to stick his cane in the spokes of bicycles when children rode them on the sidewalks. They missed Aubrey, they said. They missed him so much that they hung his cane and his chair on the wall of the Halfway Tavern. This was too delicious. It fed into all my fantasies about taverns, fantasies that had themselves been fed by stories like Hemingway's "A Good Café on the Place St-Michel." I imagined a place of hearty camaraderie, and if saucers didn't pile up on the tables to mark the quantity of brandy drunk by the patrons, surely the small empty glasses of draft beer—always ordered two at a time—were a reasonable substitute. I had to see it for myself.

It didn't take much planning. My friend Pierre was in on it from the beginning and he recruited two other men to join us. I bought a fake moustache from the Johnny Brown theatrical supply store, pinned my long hair up under a cap, and borrowed a winter jacket and gloves from Pierre. Drinking my watery draft beer was a challenge with the gloves on and I was so nervous I could barely lift my head up to look around. I'm pretty sure the waiter knew I was a woman, and I'm also pretty sure he couldn't have cared less. And the patrons—those who weren't passed out with their heads down on the sticky tables—were trying hard not to stare at my two other companions: Joel, a young Jewish mathematics professor at Concordia University, who had a very expensive camera hanging from his neck, and Gordon, a young black psychotherapist from Guyana, both of them taking an alert ethnographic interest in their surroundings. Even with my head mostly down, I could see that my grandfather's cane and chair were not hanging on the wall. Pierre approached a group of men sitting quietly in a corner. Did any of them, he asked in French, know Aubrey Cotton? They waved a little dismissively. Oh yeah, he used to drink over there with the Irish.

How do I tell the next part of this story? It seems entirely unhooked from the story of the Halfway Tavern, and yet I can't help feeling that there is some deep connection between the two, something almost revealed. Aubrey Cotton is the slender and accidental link. There was a woman at the end of his life. I never met her and the exact nature of their relationship was always unclear to me, though I had the impression they probably drank together. I clearly recall a mood of unspoken disapproval on my mother's part, but when I asked her about it recently she said the woman lived in the same apartment building as my grandfather and looked after him: "She was very good to him." But my mother's memories, even of her father, are softening and she is less quick to judgment than she was. Regardless, I somehow knew that the woman had been a cigarette girl at Rockhead's Paradise—"Montreal's smartest coloured nite club" as the advertisements had it—and I somehow knew that she was Scott Raymond's aunt.

Rockhead's was a Montreal fixture from the days when the city was wide open. Originally founded in 1928 by Rufus Rockhead, a railway porter from Jamaica who was the first Black man to be granted a tavern license in Montreal, all the great jazz musicians played there. Like so much of its working-class Little Burgundy neighbourhood, Rockhead's was torn down in the 1980s to make way for the Ville-Marie Expressway. Scott Raymond was a fixture in my life from the days of elementary school in our Montreal North neighbourhood of Ahuntsic. There he is in my kindergarten class photo, dapper in a woolen vest and white shirt. And there he is again in my grade five class photo, now the only Black kid in our predominantly white West Island school. When my family moved from the city to the suburbs, it felt like moving from one country to another where the language, the games, the expectations were different. When Scott Raymond popped up a year later, it was like seeing a long-lost compatriot, someone who understood the old ways. And there he is my high school yearbook, still handsome and serious. And there he is at the Loyola Campus of Concordia University, giving me a lift home one day, telling me about his dream of being a radio disc jockey. The car radio was on. "Look," I said, pointing out the window. "All the people are walking in time to the music." "You see that too?" he said. "I thought I was the only one."

I asked Scott once about his aunt, but he didn't answer. I assumed that she was the wild girl in her serious, aspirational family and that her association with my grandfather, whatever the relationship was, did nothing to redeem her in their eyes. I haven't seen Scott since our university days. Someone told me that he developed multiple sclerosis in his still young adulthood. But I think about him often. We move through our lives and only now and then does the breeze bring the lightest trace of the ways in which we are bound together, the pattern beneath the surface. We sniff and it's gone.

# Her Bequest

THIS MORNING, AS I EMPTIED THE DISHWASHER, I put away a plain glass salad plate, one of a set of four my grandmother gave me when a bad fall, a broken hip, and a stroke, the dreaded trifecta of old ladies everywhere, meant that she had to move from her Montreal apartment into a nursing home. Her small bequest to me also included one bone china cup and saucer and a souvenir teaspoon from Scotland. I had brought the teaspoon back for her at least twenty years earlier, when I made my first trip overseas. When she died, after too many years of every faculty but her brain shutting down, my aunt, her daughter, gave me my grandmother's photo album and a small diary in which she had recorded her 1963 honeymoon trip to Scotland and Ireland. It was a second and gentler marriage between, as I thought then, two very elderly people. I realize now with some astonishment that my grandmother was some years younger than I am now when she married Charlie Toal.

Charlie was tall, shy, very thin, bespectacled, with a shock of straight white hair. Irish Catholic, he wore woolen vests, collected stamps, and lived with his mother until she died. He was an odd choice for my grandmother, who liked a good time. Handsome rather than pretty, she was dark-haired and thick-waisted with heavy calves. She had a long face and bi-coloured eyes, the irises both blue and brown, a condition whose name, *heterochromia iridum*, sounds like a magic spell from *Harry Potter*. The flapper fashions of her young adulthood—the shingled hair, the cloche hats, the long loose jackets and coats, the strapped shoes with their low, chunky heels—suited her well and she wore them with aplomb. In a 1921 photo taken at the seaside town of Rothesay, a year or two before she left Scotland, she sits on a park bench in a three-quarter turn to the camera, legs crossed, one arm across the back of the bench, her strong face shadowed by the brim of her hat. Nineteen years old. Confident. That may have been the quality my mother, her daughter-in-law, most disliked in her, the sure confidence, against, as my mother saw it, all evidence, that she was an attractive woman and that her desires mattered.

Where did that confidence come from? Everything in her life should have conspired to wear her down. Helen Wilson Aitken Bookless was born in 1902 in Livingston, West Lothian, the fourth of five children, and christened at the Scottish Free Church in Bathgate, where she would live until she emigrated. Her father, George Bookless, was a winding engineman (or engine keeper), probably at the oil shale mines in Bathgate. Her mother, Barbara Annan, is described as a housekeeper in their 1896 marriage record. Helen, my grandmother, is listed as a hosiery worker in the June 1923 manifest of the *SS Metagama*, the ship that brought her from Glasgow to her new life in Detroit, where she joined a maternal uncle and his family. Bob Wallace, my grandfather, followed her from Bathgate to Detroit a year or two later though it's difficult to trace his movements with any accuracy. This is partly because his name is such a common one, but it's also because his relationship with the law was always a little relaxed. He entered the US illegally without a visa and, following a not uncharacteristic fight with a co-worker who then reported him to the authorities, Bob was deported. He and Helen were married in Windsor, across the river from Detroit, in 1925. It is likely that she was already pregnant with her first child and only daughter, my aunt Barbara. In a photo taken very shortly after Barbara's birth, Bob is tall, strikingly handsome and stylish, wearing his trilby hat at a jaunty angle. It's pretty clear from the photo that Bob had his eye on better things than shale mining, his father's employment, or fire building, the occupation he listed in his marriage record.

And here is where the records end and something like myth begins, a small handful of stories my father told reluctantly over the years and never with pleasure. Stories about Bob's temper and how, when he was angry with Helen, he would pull the tablecloth out from under the dinner dishes, sending everything flying. About going to the racetracks with Bob and Joe, the oldest son, and being teased for not betting enough. About Bob leaving his job in the Coca-Cola shipping department in Montreal in 1941 to "open his book"; that is, to become a bookie. But then Japan bombed Pearl Harbor, the US declared a moratorium on horse racing, and Bob went under, eventually returning to Coca-Cola. But there were also times that Bob did not return to Helen, or she to him. "This was after he and Nellie agreed to hate each other," my father told me three or four years before he died, using the name by which my grandmother was known in her immediate family. He remembered with bitterness travelling to Toronto, when he was only sixteen, to insist that she come home, only one of the times, I think, that she left Bob. It had always been clear that my father, emotionally reserved in a family of battlers and sentimentalists, didn't much like his mother. His attitude to his father may have softened at the very end. About a year before he died he told my mother, "I saw the old man last night." "Oh," she said, "how did he look?" "Pretty good," my father replied.

I have early memories of my grandmother, of course. The year, I must have been seven or eight, that she gave my father a transistor radio for Christmas. He used it to listen to the baseball games, perhaps the only passion he shared with his mother. Dinner at her apartment: roast chicken or scotch meat pies, lemon meringue pie for dessert, visiting in the small living room, then more tea and more desserts before we all went home. Plattsburgh Beach when she accompanied me to the public toilets and I saw pubic hair for the first time. Visiting her flat in the pre-Charlie days when she took in a boarder—Ina Moore, an old friend from Bathgate and a waitress at the Kresge's lunch counter—to help pay the rent.

But my abiding relationship with my grandmother really began when I left my parents' home in the suburbs and moved back to the city. I was twenty-two and she was seventy-three and I lived a few blocks away from her in the Notre-Dame-de-Grâce neighbourhood. Charlie had died three years earlier and for a few years Helen carried on in the flat she had shared with him. I would visit, usually in the afternoons, and, as I still think of it, I would learn how to be an old lady. "You have to keep busy, hen," my grandmother would say, using the familiar Scottish endearment. She remained active in her church and in her benevolent society, the Sons of Scotland. Tucked into the photo album I inherited is the program for one of their annual Burns Suppers: the welcome, the address to the haggis, the toast to the lassies, the displays of Scottish country dancing, the whole rigmarole. But what I find most evocative, evocative of a lost working-class Anglophone Montreal, is the menu which itemizes everything from the celery and olives that served as starters, to the steak pie, to the after-dinner mints. Sometimes when I visited, another old lady or two would drop by and a familiar ritual would be observed: the tablecloth would come out, along with the bone china cups and saucers; there would be scones, which my grandmother made on a hot griddle, shortbread, tea cake. On another visit, years later, keeping up with the times, she plunked a bottle of cream sherry down on the dinner table: "I know you like a bit of wine with your supper, hen."

But all this, all of it true, makes her sound like a caricature: a caricature of a Scot, a sentimental immigrant, an old lady. There were other lessons to be learned during those afternoon visits. One day she told me about seeking a divorce from Bob. "He hit me," she said bluntly. When she went to work with a black eye, she always refused to say she had walked into a door. "My husband did this me." They were living apart when Bob was diagnosed with prostate cancer and insisted on returning home to be nursed by Helen. She described making an appointment with the "top lawyer" in Montreal, the one who appeared in all the newspaper stories, only to learn from him that she would have to petition Parliament for a divorce, a lengthy and costly process prior to the 1968 national Divorce Act. In the absence of a divorce, said the lawyer, she had to take Bob back. My only memories of my grandfather, who died when I was five, are of an old man in a darkened sickroom. Today I imagine my grandmother, a waitress in the Eaton's ninth-floor dining room, sitting in the office of the "top lawyer," almost certainly a criminal lawyer if his accomplishments were widely reported in the newspapers. She would have worn her best clothes and she would have felt confident in her rights.

The hard work, the stress, nursing a man she no longer loved or even liked, all of this took its toll and, three or four years after Bob's death, Helen was admitted to the tuberculosis sanatorium in Ste. Agathe. When I asked my mother about this recently, she said "everybody was so concerned about her but she came out healthy and with a new man." My mother was always convinced that Helen married Charlie Toal for his Bell Canada pension and maybe, in part, she did. Who could blame her? In the honeymoon photographs she wears a fur stole and carries a new home movie camera. She showed Charlie off to her old friends in Bathgate, where her travel diary indicates she reaffirmed her original decision to emigrate: "Went down to see Pud Marshall at the shop & had a bag of chips while we talked to him. We had about a half hour to wait for a bus to take us up to Burns Terrace & my feet were frozen & we couldn't even get a cup of tea anywhere. They sure take in the sidewalks early in Bathgate." She played cards and drank endless cups of tea with Charlie's extended family in Portglenone, County Antrim. But her travel diary also records small tender moments like this one, on the train to Ardrossan to catch the ferry to Ireland: "My feet had been so cold in the train Charlie took my shoes off and massaged my feet."

I was eighteen or nineteen when Charlie died and the wake was held at my grandmother's flat. I remember walking past the bedroom and seeing her and Barbara, her daughter, lying on the bed, curled up, their faces close together. My grandmother was bereft and Barbara—the daughter she named after her own mother, the daughter who had become a Methodist minister and would, in a few years, take out a membership in NOW, the National Organization for Women, and march in gay rights parades—was comforting her.

In the end, Helen outlived Charlie by twenty-three years. She seldom spoke of him but they were buried together in Notre-Dame-des-Neiges Cemetery. Significantly, the cemetery's "find a grave" search engine locates her as Helen Bookless, not Helen Toal or Helen Wallace Toal. This may be an effect of the 1981 amendment to the Civil Code of Quebec, requiring married women to retain their maiden or birth names. While I imagine that my grandmother would have preferred to be known as Helen Toal, I also think that the erasure of Bob Wallace's name from her civil records would have pleased her. And I am pleased that the evocative Bookless is restored.

# White Swan, Black Swan

MY YOUNGER SISTER NANCY AND I SHARED A room until I was almost ten, which is when we moved to our four-bedroom, split-level house in the suburbs. As the eldest child, I got the only bedroom on the lower level. It was a magical room with a short, child-sized closet and a long window set at garden level. Nancy got one of the three bedrooms on the upper level; my parents of course had the master bedroom, and Catherine and Laura had to continue sharing a room until I finally moved out many years later. The unfairness of this arrangement greatly pained Catherine who begged to be allowed to make the small, windowless cold storage room her bedroom. Anything, anything for a little privacy.

A post on Facebook recently swept me back to those years of the shared bedroom. It was one of those posts from a friend/not-friend who puts up a lot of artwork by mostly very well-known artists. The kind of post you usually swipe past pretty quickly. But this image stopped me in my tracks. It was *The Swan, No. 1* painted in 1915 by Swedish artist and mystic Hilma af Klint, now often credited as the first truly abstract artist, her work predating that of Kandinsky by a handful of years. *The Swan, No. 1* is not abstract, though later work within the group of twenty-four swan images painted over two years definitely achieves a fully abstract expression. It is, though, highly stylized.

The square canvas is composed of two complementary halves, in effect one rectangle on top of another. The top half features a white swan against a black background, while the bottom half features a black swan against a white background. The white swan—wings spread and neck curving down to meet, beak to beak, the black swan—has blue feet and blue skin around its bright orange beak. The black swan's wings are similarly spread and its neck arches in the opposite direction to meet the beak of the white swan in the centre of the canvas. The tip of one wing of each of the swans also touches delicately along the horizontal axis of the painting. The image immediately evokes the well-known yin-yang symbol although the organizational geometry of *The Swan, No. 1* is more linear.

Hilma af Klint received an excellent formal training at the Royal Academy of Fine Arts in Stockholm and she made a decent living from her landscapes and portraits. But the work to which she was committed, her real work, was carried out largely in secret. Influenced by spiritualism and Theosophy, she and four other women artists—they called themselves The Five—conducted séances and communicated with supernatural High Masters who instructed Hilma af Klint to create paintings for a spiral Temple, the function of which remained mysterious. Over a nine-year period, she (or, as now seems more likely, she, together with other members of The Five, especially Anna Cassel) created 193 Temple paintings, the swan paintings among them, and produced one hundred and fifty notebooks documenting her experiences. The paintings were never exhibited during her lifetime and, in her will, Hilma af Klint instructed her beneficiary to keep the work secret for at least twenty years after her death.

Viewers and art critics now interpret *The Swan, No. 1* by emphasizing its exploration of duality and opposites: female and male, "the heavenly and the underworld," transcendence and immanence. More than one critic notes the significance of the swan in alchemy, where it "represents the union of opposites necessary for the creation of what is known as the philosopher's stone..."

But what does any of this have to do with sharing a bedroom with my sister Nancy? The reason the image stopped me in my tracks is that during those years, each of us tucked into our own bed, one of the games we played at night was White Swan, Black Swan. It is impossible now to recover the contours of the game. Basically, it was an imaginary game in which we each had a swan that we lived in, and we floated around on a lake or maybe we floated down a river. I was the oldest by two years and verbally assertive while my sister was slower to speech and more passive, so of course I got the white swan. Our swans were furnished and I think we must have described the furnishings to one another. My sister says that the swans were mostly vehicles propelling us on our adventures. I can't recall any narrative component to White Swan, Black Swan, but that may simply be the failure of memory. After all, this game makes no sense at all to the adult brain.

But thinking about it evokes that bedroom in very specific ways. We had twin beds separated by a nightstand with a lamp. There was a small handful of inexpensive children's books tucked into the nightstand. The lamp had a wavy pink plastic shade with a plastic lace overlay that always smelled dusty. The bedroom window overlooked the fourplex next door where Darlene lived with her parents, but they were really her grandparents. Monsieur Larocque played the fiddle in the kitchen in the evenings. On the long hot summer nights, the sun still up, Nancy and I lay in bed in our baby-doll pyjamas, whispering to each other and listening to sounds of life on the street. How impossible it was to sleep when the sun was still up. In the winter we would lie awake passing the White Swan, Black Swan game back and forth while the TV murmured from the living room.

Another of our games back then was more explicitly Manichean than the merely implied dualism of White Swan, Black Swan. This was Good Girl, Bad Girl. Of course, I was the good girl. This game depended on my father's dry-cleaned shirts (the cuffs starched but not the collar) which were always delivered in a stack, like a deck of cards, each of them folded around a piece of cardboard. The cardboard was, I think, a little bigger than a normal eight and a half by eleven sheet of paper and it was invitingly white. My sister and I would settle down at the kitchen table with our pencils or crayons and divide the cardboard into lengthwise quadrants, a kind of abbreviated comic book format. Good Girl got the top two rectangles and Bad Girl the bottom two. Then we would draw the various adventures and misadventures of Good Girl and her opposite, Bad Girl.

It is pretty clear from these games that I was a bossy older sister, still a little jealous of my one-time status as the only child. Looking back, though, I wonder whether Nancy wasn't allocated the imaginatively juicier role, the Satan to my self-styled Christ. After all, who wouldn't rather be the bad girl? And the black swan is the *rara avis*, the singular, the once unimaginable. The term "black swan event" entered the popular lexicon with the 2007 publication of Nassim Nicholas Taleb's book, *The Black Swan: The Impact of the Highly Improbable*. Black swan events, says Taleb, are characterized by their "rarity, extreme 'impact,' and retrospective (though not prospective) predictability." He goes on to say that a "small number of Black Swans explains almost everything in our world, from the success of ideas and religions, to the dynamics of historical events, to elements of our own personal lives."

Of course, there is nothing "black swan," or highly improbable, about an older sister consigning a younger sister to what she perceives to be an inferior role. It is entirely predictable. What is less predictable, and a little uncanny, is two little girls somehow channeling the same resonant image that inspired Hilma af Klint almost a half century earlier. Carl Jung argued that, "There are many symbols... that are not individual but *collective* in their nature and origin." The formation of such symbols or archetypes, he said, constitutes "an instinctive *trend*." Is the infant and child mind more open to receiving and forming such representations, not only in the child's dreams but in her play?

A slightly less woo-woo explanation, or partial explanation, for the emergence of the swan motif in our imaginative play might lie closer at hand. Hans Christian Andersen's story "The Wild Swans," an expanded and even baroque retelling of the Grimms' tale "The Six Swans," includes images of little Elise being carried away over the ocean in a net woven by her eleven brothers who have all been turned into wild swans by their evil stepmother. They fly so "high up in the air that the largest ship below them looked like a white sea-mew riding on the waves" and Elise sees her own shadow far below her on a great cloud. It's a magical scene and could well have inspired Nancy and me to imagine our own swans carrying us away on adventure.

But. But. But. The white and the black. Both Andersen's and Grimms' swans are resolutely white, as are the linen shirts woven of nettles that Eliza must sew and throw over the swans to return them to their human form. Woo-woo or not, it's hard not to imagine the infant mind tapping into and struggling with the great archetypal questions of duality, immanence, and transcendence, the questions themselves ferrying two little girls across the waters of the unconscious.

# Quicksand

WHEN I WAS LITTLE, DISASTER ALWAYS SEEMED both inevitable and imminent. Of course, disaster would strike. The only real question was: Would I survive, and how? I worried about the balcony falling off the front of our apartment while I stood on it, about overpasses and bridges collapsing as we drove over them, about an army of spiders emerging from beneath the radiator in our bathroom while I sat on the toilet. I worried about the atomic bomb, of course, even though our school in Montreal didn't participate in the duck-and-cover drills that were so common elsewhere. My family lived in the second-floor apartment of a fourplex and we had no basement, never mind a bomb shelter. Where, I asked, would we go when the inevitable mushroom cloud bloomed over our city? My parents tried to brush me off by saying that the Bergerons, our landlords, would take us into their basement. But I had been in their basement to play with Louise, who was my age but went to the French Catholic school. There were no provisions down there, no beds, no stockpiled canned food, no transistor radio. How long could we all last? How would we all manage? Madame Bergeron didn't speak

English and my mother didn't speak French. When they attempted conversation, which wasn't often, I sat on the front steps between them and translated. But I didn't know the French for *fallout* or *radiation poisoning*.

Almost as alarming as the inevitability of atomic war was the possibility of quicksand. Quicksand was everywhere in the cowboy and adventure movies and television shows of the late 1950s and early 1960s, from the lowest of the lowbrow to David Lean's *Lawrence of Arabia* and Hiroshi Teshigahara's *Woman in the Dunes*. Quicksand could be masked under a carpet of dead leaves on a forest floor or found on the edge of a Louisiana bayou. Or, even more mysteriously and insidiously, it could lie invisibly in the middle of a desert or on the high plains of Wyoming. "Hey, kid! Quicksand! Get back, get back! C'mon, reach me something! C'mon kid, get me a branch or something!" The sucking, grasping morass pulls its victim down, until only a single hand reaches pathetically for air, for something—anything—to hold onto before it, too, disappears beneath the inscrutable surface.

Victims of quicksand were almost unfailingly noble as they sank fatefully down, pleading with their companions to retreat, to save themselves, until the last slow air bubble broke the thick surface. I, too, reached for nobility in my one anticlimactic encounter with quicksand. We had just moved to our new, still-in-progress suburban development. Our neighbourhood bordered building sites and farmers' fields and small stands of woods with abandoned cabanes à sucre and, once, thrillingly, a cow's skull. For the first time in our up-until-then-urban lives we wore tall rubber billy boots as we explored our new environment. One day, a couple of little sisters tagging along, I ventured a half mile or so in the direction of fields. The terrain here was broken, muddy, scattered with discarded boards, bricks, paint cans, old tarps. Proud of my new billy boots I stepped into the middle of a large brown puddle and... I was stuck, panic stricken, the thick clay mud trapping me. "It's quicksand!" I called out, terrified, to the other two. "Get help!" One of my sisters began to cry, the other looked around, unsure, in this non-urban landscape, which way was home. I tugged and tugged, the mud sucked and slurped, and suddenly my foot came free... of my boot. The quicksand was clearly less interested in my foot than my boot, because somehow, I hobbled stocking footed through the mud and we all made our way home. The fate of my boot is lost to memory but not the feeling that anything could happen in that strange, unsidewalked place.

It was around then that I had recurring nightmares of falling into quicksand. These nightmares were always associated with the jerking motion—hypnagogic or myoclonic jerks—that sometimes happen as one is falling asleep. I don't know if the jerk prompted the dream, or the dream prompted the jerk. Regardless, it would wake me up before I sank irretrievably down. It wasn't very much later that the quicksand nightmare was replaced by the Nazi nightmare. By now we had a house and the house had a basement and the basement is where I hid when the Nazis came, making myself small beneath the open wooden steps, their boots stomping down those steps as I watched and held my breath. That was pretty much the whole of the dream because then my pounding heart would wake me up. Why Nazis? They were probably as ubiquitous on TV as quicksand. And maybe by then I was reading *The Diary of Ann Frank*. But this nightmare, which recurred for years, felt less anticipatory, less like something that could happen than like something that *had* happened. For years I held, privately, the conviction that these dreams were uncanny memories of a former life. It's hard to shake that feeling, even now, though I'm also inclined to see it as the sleeping mind tapping into the historical nightmare of the collective unconscious.

While atomic warfare, quicksand, and genocidal Nazism might not be clear and present dangers, they were at least impersonal. If any of those disasters befell me, it wouldn't be my fault. I might be a victim, but I wouldn't be guilty of anything. But another vague worry of my childhood went in a different direction. What if I ended up in prison? It could happen. This worry is more complicated and it interests me because it suggests a kind of wobbliness, or unpredictability, not just in the world but in myself. I could end up in prison either because of some caprice, some unpredictable glitch in the social system, a mistake, or because of something I had done. I was the kind of child who, like George Washington, *couldn't* tell a lie, but who's to say I *wouldn't* commit a heinous crime? I *couldn't* tell a lie, which suggests something like a moral compass but also a degree of personal helplessness. I couldn't tell a lie, even when it might be in my clear self-interest, and so maybe I *would* commit a crime, which would also be against my ultimate self-interest. As a child, I was less anxious about the crime or the conviction than the consequence. What would prison be like? Would I have to use the toilet in front of other people? Would I stand on tiptoe to look out the tiny window and yearn for the fields beyond? Would I scratch lines into the wall of my cell and count off the weeks? Would I have to eat slop?

I might once have assumed that, as a child, my sense of self was unstable and a bit of a mystery to me, and that would account for the feeling that I could possibly end up in prison. But now that I have much less life ahead of me than behind

me, I see that wobbliness and instability are the real founda-
tions of self, everything else an illusion. Things can happen in
a split second. The world can split open in a split second. You
can be overcome, by someone else or by your own self. A moment's distraction and your car strikes the child in the cross-
walk. Suddenly you're a different person. Or, as happened
to me when my first marriage was breaking down, you get
into your car and drive to work in a different city, suddenly
realizing that your brakes are very, very soft. Did he do this?
Was he that desperate for the new woman, the new life? The
feeling lasts a second, a split second, but in that second the
world shifts a little on its axis. This happens, you think, this
is how it happens.

# Caesar Salad

TODAY I DRAPED A PASHMINA SCARF ACROSS MY desk, gold-coloured, paisley-patterned, a gift from one of my sisters. I did this to protect the finish of the desk, which was becoming marred where my bare arms rest on it as I type at my laptop. Of course, it is not a true pashmina scarf, not the kind of cashmere pashmina that movie stars carry with them on long flights to exotic locations, wrapping it around thin shoulders or bundling it under stylishly tousled heads. And that is okay because I am not really the kind of girl who drapes scarves over things, though I have always wanted to be. The kind of girl who throws a patterned silk scarf insouciantly over the ugly lamp in the cheap motel room where she is staying with her lover, her gesture instantly transforming the room into an *Arabian Nights* seraglio. An Anaïs Nin kind of girl, draping scarves over things and writing long journal entries about her affair with her psychoanalyst.

Or maybe even a Patti Smith kind of girl, though scarf aesthetics don't seem to play a big part in her biker-jacketed, cowboy-booted, long-grey-haired world. Patti Smith does what she wants to, and gestures that would seem fey if performed by anyone else accumulate a definite halo when performed by Patti Smith—remembering birthdays, always birthdays; posting a detail, from a fifteenth century painting, of the stigmata on the risen Christ's feet on her Instagram site on Easter morning; making pilgrimages to Arthur Rimbaud's grave, or taking Polaroid photos of Sylvia Plath's grave in the snow. Years and years later she will return to Plath's grave, whispering to it "I have come back, Sylvia." Once she journeyed all the way to French Guiana to bring home three stones from the now abandoned Devil's Island penal colony of Saint-Laurent-du-Maroni. Her plan was to present the stones to Jean Genet who had so fervently desired to serve his sentence there, in that place of "inviolable criminality." But history deprived Genet of Devil's Island, closed by the French government before he could be exiled there, just as it would deprive Patti Smith of Genet who died before she could reach him. She had to satisfy herself by making a pilgrimage to his Moroccan grave and burying the stones there. Patti Smith is big on pilgrimages. She follows her own nose.

Following your own nose was not a habit that was encouraged in my family, where it was regarded as form of suspect cultural aspiration. Moderate or decorous social aspiration was one thing—the right golf club, the right neighbourhood, even the right tailor. Cultural aspiration was something else altogether. It smacked of taking yourself seriously, or drawing attention to yourself, or, worst of all, maybe, being yourself. But every now and then one of us made a stab at it. Once it was my father. One day in the mid-1960s he arrived home, to our new home in the suburbs, carrying a teak salad bowl set: one large bowl, six little ones, and matching serving spoons.

It was the heyday of teak. Even so, this gesture was surprising. My father was not a shopper, so it's possible he was given the salad bowl set as a gift. But he also brought home the recipe for the Queen Elizabeth Hotel Caesar salad, and that weekend he set himself to making the salad. The recipe would have been that of the famous Beaver Club, the hotel's steak-and-martini mecca in the heart of the business district, newly relocated from the narrow streets of Old Montreal to the enormous cruciform tower of Place Ville Marie, then the tallest skyscraper in the Commonwealth. My father's ambition was to make a true Caesar salad. This meant preparing it tableside with all the appropriate flourishes. As he proceeded, every element in the Caesar salad struck us as wildly, and perhaps dangerously, exotic. Anchovies! Garlic! A raw egg! Croutons! Romaine lettuce, so different from our usual iceberg! I cannot at all recall what we thought of the salad, or even whether we kids were willing to eat it, but I recall clearly the atmosphere of anxious theatre. Could he pull it off?

Now I wonder what was at stake for him. I puzzle over this episode, which seems so uncharacteristic. Aside from manning the barbeque—in those days a small, round charcoal briquette barbeque dedicated to hot dogs and hamburgers—I don't remember him making anything else. He did, especially later, after we had all left home, like to make the cocktails when he and my mother had guests. Another singular occasion sticks in my memory like a burr. My Uncle Joe, newly permitted back into the family circle after years of probably deserved exile, was visiting with his flashily glamorous partner Pauline. Pauline of the big hair, big voice, big jewelry. Pauline who unexpectedly charmed everyone, even shy Methodist minister Uncle Harold, who was also there. My father made the drinks but, instead of adding water to the glasses of scotch whiskey at the kitchen sink, his usual practice, he put a little jug of water on a tray with the drinks and carried the whole thing out to the living room where he added water to Joe and Pauline's glasses to their taste. Part of me wanted to tease him about this unexpected formality. Another part of me wanted to cry. It was such a small gesture on my father's part but even now it seems to carry a weight that I cannot understand. I don't think it had to do with Joe or Pauline or family dynamics. I think it was the kind of small gesture, like the Caesar salad, that opens a door onto a world of unrealized longing, or maybe only partially realized longing.

How do you go about inhabiting the world you imagine for yourself? What magic, what combination of words and gestures will bring it into being? For my father, maybe there were two worlds. The downtown world that, for him, was increasingly a world of sharp suits and business lunches and executive secretaries. Every day he left this world and walked through Place Ville Marie, past the Queen Elizabeth Hotel, and down the escalator into Central Station to catch the commuter train home where four pairs of sticky little hands were waiting to greet him. Which man was he? Which man was he allowed to be? Where did his nose want to take him? All I know is that he carried his nose a long way from the Christophe-Colomb Avenue apartment of his youth.

And now it is 1978. I have moved to Toronto, a city whose wide streets I find alien and unsympathetic, and I am sitting in a movie theatre watching the Philip Kaufman remake of *Invasion of the Body Snatchers*, starring Donald Sutherland, Brooke Adams, Leonard Nimoy, Jeff Goldblum, Veronica Cartwright. Have I ever wanted to inhabit a world more than that one? Something about it called to me in the same way that Caesar salad called to my father. Not the body snatching, of course; not the takeover by little alien seed blobs blown to earth by solar winds. What I wanted was the green, green world of twisty quirky San Francisco before the property boom, before the entrepreneurs, and before venture capital. I wanted Brooke Adams's house, all vintage lace curtains and houseplants. I wanted her relationship with Donald Sutherland, her dear colleague, her ironic equal. I wanted their quirky circle of friends, psychiatrists and mud bath operators. What I would get, for a little while at least, was Geoffrey, Brooke Adams's dentist husband, handsome and bland, the first to fall victim—willing victim?—to the alien takeover. And what a takeover. The alien seed blobs insinuate themselves into the green world, morphing into giant pulsating plant larvae, horrible fetal copies of their host humans, eventually supplanting them completely.

Patti Smith would never have been duped by Geoffrey the dentist. Her unfailing nose would have sniffed him out long before the solar winds unmasked him. But as I write this, I am sitting at my desk looking out at a green, green world. It isn't perfect. The tiny green caterpillars that will become winter moths have been especially voracious this year, and the leaves of the Garry oaks hang like delicate, fragile lace. But a scarf is draped across my desk, my dog is sleeping in the chair behind me, and my dear colleague and ironic equal is talking to himself in the next room.

# Mean Girls

THE 2004 FILM *MEAN GIRLS* IS A COMEDIC anthropology of high school culture from the perspective of one teenage girl. Sixteen-year-old Cady Heron, the home-schooled child of research zoologists, who has spent the last twelve years of her life in "Africa" (no more specific location is offered), enters a mainstream school for the first time. It is, she says, "like leaving the actual world and entering girl world." And "girl world [has] a lot of rules." Taken in hand initially by Janis Ian, a goth artist, and her gay friend Damien, Cady is given a hand-drawn map of the school's various tribes as they position themselves around the school cafeteria. There are the Preps, the Jocks, the Asian Nerds, the Cool Asians, the Unfriendly Black Hotties, the Girls Who Eat Their Feelings, the Girls Who Don't Eat Anything, the Desperate Wannabes, the Burnouts, the Sexually Active Band Geeks, the Art Freaks. And then there are The Plastics, otherwise known as Teen Royalty, three privileged white girls whose leader Regina (aka The Queen Bee) is routinely crowned Spring Fling Queen in the school competition. In Regina, says Janis, "evil takes a human form." The attractive and naïve Cady is, as teen movie narrative demands, invited to sit at The Plastics' cafeteria table where she is initiated into their rules: "On Wednesdays we wear pink"; "You can't wear a tank top two days in a row and you can only wear a ponytail once a week." Most crucially, "Ex-boyfriends are off limits to friends. That's just, like, the rules of feminism!" Inevitably, mayhem ensues. Cady develops a crush on Regina's ex-boyfriend. She is recruited by goth artist Janis to infiltrate The Plastics and undermine their hegemony. "[In] girl world," says Cady, "all the fighting had to be sneaky." But rather than undermining The Plastics, she finds herself seduced by the power they exercise. "Being with The Plastics was like being famous. People looked at you all the time and everybody just knew stuff about you." Cady loses herself and behaves badly. She finds herself again and makes restitution. She is, predictably, crowned Spring Fling Queen.

*Mean Girls* is a hyperbolic representation of high school culture, but aspects ring true to me. When, in grade four, I moved from an inner-city Montreal elementary school to a suburban school, a couple of things were immediately apparent. First, the student body was less diverse. In the city, I hung around mostly with the two Japanese girls in my class, Judy and Joan. We called ourselves The Three Js. My mother remembers us being invited to the house of one of the girls for a tea ceremony. And I had a crush on Dennis Khouri who I think was Persian, as we said then. Or he might have been Lebanese. He was a small dapper boy who, in class photos, wears a woolen vest over a white shirt and tie. The student body at suburban Westpark School was overwhelmingly white, including a handful of Jewish students and a French Canadian. The French Canadian, bad boy Marc Lavoie, failed French because he refused to speak anything other than a Quebec *joual*, offending our mostly North African French teachers. Aside from the overwhelming whiteness and middle classness of the student body, there was also a new vocabulary. On my first day in my new classroom, I was told to sit at the desk of a girl who was sick at home. I can't remember her name, so I'll call her Susan. Another student leaned over to me and whispered, "Susan is very popular." Popular? A new concept. I filed it away. At my old school students could possibly be divided by those who paid for their milk at lunch time and those who got their milk for free, though even that didn't seem to be a big deal. But popularity was clearly a very big deal at Westpark School.

Our large comprehensive high school must have had some of the same tribes as those identified in *Mean Girls*, but I remember only two: the smokers and the juicers. The smokers smoked weed and dropped acid and hung out at the Dairy Queen, and the juicers drank liquor and hung out at the pizzeria. The smokers cultivated a cool irony while the juicers went in for a rougher humour. The two solitudes of Quebec recreated in teenage microcosm. For most of my time in high school I floated between tribes, not feeling any need or desire for affiliation. I hung out with different girls at different times, dated different boys at different times. It wasn't until late in my final year that I became very loosely associated with the smokers because I fell in love with one of them.

I see now that in both high school and elementary school, I always managed to remain successfully unaffiliated, a free agent. I was never lonely, never picked on. I never had a clique or a gang, but I always had friends. But, of course, others were not so lucky and over the years—no, over the decades—I have been haunted by my part in perpetuating what must have been the misery of a handful of my fellow students.

My part was almost always, I think, a sin of omission, not a sin of commission, but a sin nonetheless. A cowardice.

The person I am most haunted by is Mary Smith. My friend Gaby remembers her showing up in our grade four or five suburban classroom and then disappearing after that. We somehow knew that she was adopted, though Mary Smith seems a cruelly anonymous name to give an adopted child. I remember her as big for her age. Her regulation school tunic fit snugly and awkwardly and her dark hair was cut bluntly. Gaby remembers that our teacher "went out of her way to be mean to Mary," and we happily followed her example, making a playground game of passing around Mary's "cooties," none of us wanting to be infected by those imaginary germs. I have a vague memory of Mary spinning around in the schoolyard, fending off our small assaults, though it's possible this is not the memory of a real event but a scene from a movie. It doesn't really matter. There is emotional truth in the memory regardless of whether it's real or imagined. It was some years ago that it suddenly occurred to me that Mary was a First Nations child, almost certainly adopted, or maybe fostered, during the now infamous sixties scoop. I don't think we children could have known that she was First Nations, or Indian, as we would have said then. It's extremely unlikely that any of us had ever knowingly *met* a First Nations person, in spite of the fact that the large Kahnawake Mohawk reserve was on the South Shore, directly across from Montreal. But Mary's difference, her awkward vulnerability, made her a target. And although I would not have instigated the cruel goading, I probably participated. I know that I did not intervene and I am left with the shameful image of Mary Smith's terrible isolation.

It wasn't only girls who picked on Mary Smith and there was then nothing "sneaky" about our cruelty. We got sneakier as we got older. In our early years at high school we kind of picked on Deborah McTavish who was thin and flat as a board, with flaming red hair. But our way of picking on her was so subtle that I'm not sure she ever knew. My friend Gaby remembers Deborah in the shower room after gym class, stripping down and walking into the showers, her flat, little girl's body pale white and straight shouldered. She didn't seem to know that such unselfconsciousness was a no-no, it broke the rules. You were supposed to fade away and refuse to shower, or shower in your underwear or do your best to hide behind the skimpy towel. In spite of her oddness, Deborah was a curiously confident girl with an enormous and precocious vocabulary that she revelled in. She had an unusual skipping way of walking and Marianne Simard, who was herself galumphy but so aggressive that no one dared pick on her, mimicked Deborah's walk in the hallways. And we all laughed at Deborah's curiously adult erudition. I guess the meanest thing we did was pretend to sympathize with her about the teasing she got and then, among ourselves, laugh at her afterward.

Gaby recently recovered, maybe in an old yearbook, a prize-winning little essay that Deborah wrote in grade eight. It's an apocalyptic piece called "The End of the World" and it describes "slow, deliberate... monsters, bent on destroying the human race." But, by a miracle, the people are "taken up" by God whose voice concludes the essay: "Lo, these are My beloved children, with whom I am well pleased." I think there are a couple of ways to read this essay. The first suggests that Deborah was not as oblivious to our contempt as she seemed, that we were the "slow, deliberate monsters."

The second, by which I am more persuaded, suggests that Deborah grew up in a religious household and that she was a much-loved child in a cohesive community of adults, and this is what underlay her confidence and her ability to walk her own path... albeit skippingly.

Deborah McTavish left our school after a year or two and I don't know what became of her. But I do know what became of another girl from a zealously religious household. I know because I Googled her. Frances Vaughan was not so much teased or picked on as completely ignored, in a way, shunned. Her crime was piety, as indicated by the ambition she contributed to her yearbook entry: "To serve God." I hung out with her for a couple of weeks one summer and she initiated me into a game of her own invention. We filled test-tube–type containers with milk—in hindsight, I think they must have been containers for vanilla bean pods—to which we added a bit of vanilla extract. We sipped the concoction and careened around, pretending to be drunk. I much later learned that there is a small amount of alcohol in vanilla extract. How could Frances come up with such a game? What, in her home life, could have prompted it? More alarmingly, she told me that she and her father slept in the same bed. She spoke disapprovingly of her mother who was known, among the neighbourhood bridge club set, to be a little too attractive, a little too sexy. My friendship with Frances was a matter of days but I never forgot her.

I didn't know what to expect when I Googled her, but what I discovered was a full and meaningful life well lived. She went on to complete a PhD in theology at McGill University, publishing a couple of frequently cited articles as an independent scholar. She moved to the country near Kingston, Ontario with her Mennonite husband, and eventually supported one of her two daughters, a future Green Party candidate, in their transition from being Caitlin to being Calvin. She has two massive dogs and has written a book in support of animal welfare. Her father's obituary (he died five years ago) indicates that he was predeceased by two wives and had numerous grandchildren and great-grandchildren. It says nothing about him as a person.

What is one to make of all this? It's difficult to imagine that Mary Smith met with as much loving success in life, but of course I could be wrong. And surely it would be as wrong to imagine her doomed by her background as it was to torment her because of what we intuited of her background.

When I think of Mary Smith (it seems impossible to disarticulate those two almost hackneyed generic names), I also recall the Today's Child columns that ran in Canadian newspapers from the mid-1960s to the early 1980s. The column, effectively an advertisement, was intended to help place the "hard to adopt." First Nations and Métis children were disproportionately represented. Many survivors of the sixties scoop describe the ads as akin to those posted by dog rescue societies. But, as a teenager and young adult, I read the columns avidly, studying the black and white photo portraits of the children. They were invariably neatly dressed, the little boys in bow ties, their hair newly trimmed; the girls in ponytails or pigtails, or sometimes in the short, blunt style worn by Mary Smith. Their expressions were sometimes serious, sometimes shyly excited at having their photos taken. I imagined that one day I might adopt one of them, offering him or her a stable and loving home. I don't think I imagined the interiority of the children themselves; I certainly didn't imagine what the loss of a culture might mean to them. I didn't imagine them alone in a schoolyard, their cooties being passed from one jeering child to another. Even now, I can locate Deborah and Frances, at least imaginatively, in a social and familial context, but Mary Smith floats, unanchored.

# The Light Princess

I WAS IN MY THIRTIES THE FIRST TIME I READ George MacDonald's *The Light Princess* in preparation for teaching an undergraduate course on varieties of fairy tale. Published in 1864, the novella-length book is based loosely on "The Sleeping Beauty." The king and queen have long wanted a child. When the baby finally arrives, the king neg-lects to invite his own sister to the christening. Unfortunately, his sister is a witch. She makes her way to the event regardless and manages to throw something into the baptismal font water while muttering this curse: "Light of spirit, by my charms, / Light of body, every part, / Never weary human arms— / Only crush thy parents' heart!"

The effect of the curse is immediately apparent when the nurse cannot feel the now weightless baby in her arms. The wicked aunt "had deprived the child of all her gravity." Before long the baby is floating up to the ceiling, or out the window, or being tossed back and forth by the servants like a helium balloon. But the princess's lack of gravity is not only physical. She has no emotional or moral gravity, constantly bursting out into inappropriate fits of laughter: "... only in her laugh there was something missing.... I think it was a certain tone, depending upon the possibility of sorrow."

It is only when she is immersed or swimming in the nearby lake that the princess regains something approaching gravity. The lake becomes "the passion of her life."

Inevitably, a prince enters the story. In search of a suitable princess, the prince finds himself passing through a forest where he soon encounters the princess in the lake. Assuming that she is drowning, he jumps in to rescue her. As he lifts her onto the bank, she begins to float away, finally catching herself on a tree. In spite of her odd handicap, the prince falls in love with her and soon they are meeting secretly to swim nightly in the lake. For her part, the princess, lacking gravity, is incapable not only of falling in love, but of understanding the very concept of love.

Their nightly idyll is disrupted when it becomes clear that the water level in the lake is sinking. The wicked aunt, learning of the princess's pleasure in swimming, has effectively pulled the plug on it. Not satisfied with draining the lake, she goes on to dry up every source of water in the kingdom. What is to be done?

A gold plate is discovered at the bottom of the empty lake, engraved on it the following words: "Death alone from death can save. / Love is death, and so is brave— / Love can fill the deepest grave. / Love loves on beneath the wave." A sacrifice is required. "The body of a living man could alone stanch the flow." The prince offers himself as a kind of human cork, on one condition. While he sits in the hole at the bottom of the lake, awaiting drowning as the lake replenishes, the princess must feed him with her own hand and look at him now and then. Initially indifferent to his plight, the princess suddenly becomes frantic as the water begins to cover his face. She jumps into the water and rescues him. Back in her room, she bursts into tears and falls to the floor. Love has restored her gravity.

I read *The Light Princess* in the 1969 edition hauntingly illustrated by Maurice Sendak. When the princess discovers the joy of water, Sendak shows her floating on her back, drifting by clumps of reeds, very like John Everett Millais's painting of Ophelia, an image that evokes the potential tragedy of her situation. His depiction of the scene in which the princess gazes down into the eyes of the prince, by now up to his neck in water, holding in her hands a biscuit clearly shaped like a communion wafer and a small goblet of wine, makes explicit the Christ-like sacrifice of the prince.

But, more than the illustrations, what really stopped me in my tracks on my initial reading was the premise of the story. A child who has no gravity, who can't help floating up to the ceiling. Where had I heard that before? From my mother, about Great Aunt Amy.

Amy Sutton was not an aunt by blood. She entered the family circle when my maternal grandfather, Aubrey Cotton, boarded at her house sometime after he returned from the First World War. Amy's boarding house was in Drummond-ville, a town about a hundred kilometres east of Montreal. I asked my mother why her father didn't return to his family home, a short distance away. She said his was a very large and a very poor family. There probably wasn't room for him, and he doubtless assumed he'd eat better at Amy's. Not only were there fewer mouths to feed, but she was an excellent cook. Amy developed an enormous affection and respect for my grandfather, seeking his advice on matters of consequence. This surprises me a little. My grandfather was perhaps five foot two, a mostly unemployed carpenter. But her regard for him was matched on his side, and they maintained a close relationship until his death.

From the slender beginning of the boarding house, Amy became a member of the family, and I grew up on stories about her. How she was well off, coming from an arm of the Pears soap family. How, a nurse during the war, she emigrated to Canada with her then husband, Alf Sutton, a womanizer who absconded shortly after. How she had her deceased pet cat, Blackie, stuffed by a taxidermist. Blackie lay eternally on a pillow in his wicker basket in the kitchen. How my mother was sent to live with Amy for several weeks while the polio epidemic, which crippled and even killed so many children, raged in Montreal. Amy had by then moved to a farm in Saint-Polycarpe where she and her permanent lodger, Ted Checkland, almost certainly her lover, kept cows and a horse and wagon. Ted would deliver the big cans of milk to the local dairy. My mother loved the horse and Ted finally gave in to her pleading that she be allowed to take the reins. My mother says the horse turned but the wagon didn't, and they ended up in the ditch.

By the time I knew Great Aunt Amy, as my sisters and I called her, she was an old woman, stout with a warty face. When Ted died, Amy moved to the east end of Montreal and visited us a handful of times a year, a habit she kept up when we moved to the West Island. Once she took my whole family out for lunch to celebrate my mother's birthday, my very first time eating in a restaurant. It struck me as enormously glamourous, but my mother tells me the restaurant was the quite modest Murray's, a chain best known for its tea and steamed fruit pudding. Amy presented my mother with an amethyst ring. The ring was not her most extravagant gift. One of my cousins was born with no legs below the knees, perhaps, though I'm not sure, a victim of thalidomide. He was a clever and ambitious boy, but his family was not well off. When Amy learned that he was taking piano lessons, she bought a piano and had it delivered to their apartment.

Amy's actions and visits were always unpredictable. When we were little and there were only three of us, she showed up with three pretty dresses, each of which fit perfectly. When I was in my late teens, she arrived at our suburban home laden with items she clearly considered precious. Among them was a four-person set of cutlery which she said was made of gold. The cutlery was certainly the colour of gold, more golden than gold, each place setting packaged in plastic. It looked like a promotional giveaway from a gas station. Nonetheless, I happily accepted the knives, forks, and spoons and used them in my first apartment. There was a tin tea caddy with an attractive floral design. I kept that until we downsized five years ago. Most movingly, she brought a small black and white photo of a First World War officer, dapper in his cap and pencil moustache. Amy cried as she explained that this was her fiancé, who died, not in battle, but of a fishbone stuck, she said, in his rectum. I don't think my sisters and I had ever heard the word rectum spoken aloud before. Nor had I spent time with an adult whose feelings were so close to the surface and so simply expressed. Along with the gold cutlery and the tea caddy, I kept the officer's photo for many years. The whole atmosphere at our kitchen table that day suggested that Amy, preparing for death, was distributing precious elements of her estate. But she would go on to live another decade, dying at the great age of ninety-eight. By then my parents had left Quebec and had been living in the Toronto area for a half-dozen years, and my mother had fallen out of touch with Amy. She always found Amy uncomfortably odd and was, I think, glad to abandon the relationship.

To my mind, here is the most startling thing about stout, warty Great Aunt Amy. It's the story she told my mother and her two sisters when they were little, a story my mother later related to me several times. It was about how, when she was a child, Amy couldn't stay on the ground. She would float up to the ceiling. Even now, when she repeats this story to me, my mother emphasizes that Amy seemed to really believe it. In my mother's words, Amy was convinced that she floated and that it was a real problem for her. I never heard anything about when or how she overcame that difficulty. By the time I knew her, she was firmly fixed to the floor.

Obviously, my mother's memory of Amy's story is that of a credulous child. Every indication is that Amy came from a well-to-do family from whom she had inherited some money. Presumably she had a reasonably good education; if not an extensive formal education, then at least the kind of education that would have exposed her to children's books like those of George MacDonald. I have no doubt that Amy knew exactly what she was doing when she told my mother and her sisters the story of her own lack of gravity. The surprising thing is how much the story has haunted two generations of women, my mother and me.

I STRUGGLED TO FIND A WAY TO FINISH THIS PIECE about Great Aunt Amy. I tried meditating on the social disappearance of honorary aunts and great aunts. I tried thinking about whether the past was more tolerant of eccentricities and unconventional relationships than we give it credit for.

I tried describing my mother's childhood on Jeanne Mance Street in Montreal and locating Amy in that complicated milieu. Nothing was working. But why did it matter? Why does Amy matter to me? I think it has to do with the much-loved black cat, the cat she couldn't let go. It's the weeping over a long-dead fiancé. It's the story she told, in all seriousness, hoping to amuse, or at least intrigue, three bewildered little girls. These details kept her vividly alive in my imagination.

The problem was Amy's Mary Poppins-like appearance and disappearance from our family narrative. Like Mary Poppins, she seemed detached from her own background, floating in some middle space between beginnings and endings. She had no children and if she maintained contact with her family in England, we didn't know about it. I wondered: will I be one of the last people to hold her in memory? To remember her oddness and her strangely compelling self-assurance?

On to Google. I finally came up with the right search term—British nurses First World War—and aspects of Amy's life opened before my eyes. A page in the National Archives (UK) site was devoted to "British Army nurses' service records 1914–1918." A couple more links and there they were: fifty pages of forms and reports dedicated to Amy Pear. She trained as a nurse at the Derbyshire Royal Infirmary from 1907, when she would have been about twenty-two years old, until 1910, after which she worked as a private nurse at the Royal Hospital in Portsmouth. She must have joined up with the Territorial Force Nursing Service (TFNS) as soon as war was declared, and by December 1914 she was in France. She spent two years there, primarily in Calais, working as a surgical and medical nurse in charge of a floor of seventy-two beds, before she was transferred (after only two weeks leave) to the 5TH Southern General Hospital in Portsmouth, where the patients included not only wounded British and Belgian, but German soldiers. She served there until she was demobilized in March 1919. The annual reports by her superiors are overwhelmingly positive and in 1915 she was promoted to the rank of Sister. In April 1919 she was awarded the Royal Red Cross, Second Class, a military decoration for exceptional services in military nursing.

As always, the more one learns, the more questions pop up. My grandfather was stationed in France during the war. Is it possible that he made initial contact with Amy then? She maintained her maiden name throughout her correspondence with the TFNS and the War Office, correspondence that continued into the 1930s. Was this because regulations meant that, as a married woman after the war, she would have been required to resign? Her continuing membership meant a lot to her, and she left the TFNS only when age and health meant that she would not be able to serve if called up.

●─●─●

IN MOST WAYS, THERE WAS NOTHING "LIGHT" about Amy Pear Sutton. My mother thought of her as "an odd duck," gruff, serious. Not at all the kind of person who lacked gravity. But I like to think that the admirable and unconventional life she made for herself, floating away from all the expectations she must have felt as a woman of her time and class, gave her a certain buoyant lightness of being.

# MIDDLE

# The Back River

DURING MY EARLY YEARS IN MONTREAL, OUR little street of fourplexes and walk-up apartment buildings was just one block away from the busy intersection of Boulevard Henri Bourassa and Boulevard St. Laurent. It was four blocks from Rivière des Prairies, always known, by Anglo Montrealers, as the Back River. Despite its nominally secondary and relative status, the Back River was a bigger part of our lives than the St. Lawrence River, which, at that time, was still bordered by the old Irish slum districts of Pointe St-Charles and Griffintown, the as yet ungentrified Old Port, and the largely industrial neighbourhoods of Hochelaga and Maisonneuve.

The Back River ran like a spine through my childhood and adolescence. We followed its course, albeit swimming against its west to east current, when we moved from Montreal north to our West Island suburb. The river was there waiting for me, across the railroad tracks and then across a couple of undeveloped fields behind the high school I later attended. Those fields were the scene of some of my earliest sexual adventures, itchy in the tall grass and full of the buzzing and humming of insects. At night the same fields were dark and loud with crickets.

The Back River was (and still is) a dirty river, its shoreline often clogged with used condoms and other detritus washed out from the city's toilets. But it could also be a place of unexpected prettiness. One of my earliest memories is of being on a path, a paved asphalt path, by the river with my mother and one or two of my three younger sisters. The path falls away on one side and the ground there is covered with tall, bright blue flowers. The stamens are pink and pronounced and the stems are bristly, impossible to pick. As we stand admiring the flowers, an old man—he speaks no English, my mother speaks no French—takes out his penknife and his handkerchief, cuts a small bouquet, and presents it to my mother. She is twenty-three or twenty-four, slim and pretty. I know now that the flowers were viper's bugloss (*Echium vulgare*), also known as blueweed. The plant was once said to be a remedy against snakebites and is prized now for its ability to attract bees.

The Back River stood in for nature in our north end, highly urban neighbourhood but our excursions there were few. Four blocks are a world away for short legs. Aside from the river, nature took the form of trees, maples that dropped their helicopter seed pods every spring. Mushrooms grew at the base of some of these trees and an Englishman down the street picked them to cook and eat. There was a rabbit foot key chain in the window of the corner store. How I coveted that key chain, how I longed to carry that totemic bit of animal, to stroke it whenever I liked. Once, shockingly, there was a dead moose on the back of a car, the young hunter taking a saw to its neck. People on the street gathered to examine it and to hear the boasts of the man who shot it. Walking home, my father remarked—apropos of what?—that the hunter, who may not have been out of his teens, was awfully young to need a full set of dentures.

But every now and then a bit of vacant lot in our neighbourhood could also produce, with an unexpected flourish, a small miracle. Once it was a milkweed pod, brown and open, full of unimaginably silky seed clusters, softer and more delicate than dandelion puffs. Another time it was a praying mantis (*Mantis religiosa*), which I caught and kept, but only briefly, in a jar. These events still glow in my memory, that part of my memory that speaks in the second person. "Remember when you found the milkweed pod?" So singular in its soft seeded beauty. "Remember when you found the praying mantis?" So unmatched in its green and ancient elegance. It was a world of the unique, the unrepeatable.

A new world of nature opened up when we moved to our suburban neighbourhood, newly scraped out of a small village and its adjacent farmland. This was a rough and tumble world, still in its birth throes: discarded paint cans and building materials where lawns would eventually dominate; backhoes and dump trucks deserted for the weekend; partially completed houses and brand new sewer lines to climb down and explore. "I buried a peanut butter jar under your closet," says a friend who moved there before us and claims to have scrambled around our unfinished house. This seems so implausible that it might be true. There are tadpoles in the standing water of newly dug out basements, and mice nesting in abandoned construction tarps. But, best of all, there are fields and woods, as yet undeveloped, only a couple of rambling unpaved blocks away from home.

We crossed one field and came to a wooden fence and an old water pump. How did we know to prime that pump with standing water from the old cattle trough? We crossed another field and came to our tree. The tree. "We're going to the tree," we would tell our mothers, who were mostly preoccupied and incurious. The tree was an ancient weeping willow (*Salix babylonica*). One large branch had broken away and lay—still live, still growing—along the ground. We scrambled up that branch and perched in the tree, eating our sandwiches and plotting. We plotted how to build a log bridge to a nearby bit of raised land that was surrounded by water, nothing more than run-off. The island. The bridge. We crossed another field and came to a creek running beneath a culvert. We thought we saw small tracks in the mud. The creek. We took our shoes off and waded. We crossed the culvert and went into the woods where we kicked up an old cow skull buried beneath the leaves. We followed the path to an abandoned and primitive maple sugar shack, empty but for a couple of rusting vats and buckets. The maple sugar shack.

This was the pattern of our summer.

A couple of years later I went back to the fields, back to the tree, walking with a friend who shared my name though she spelled hers more conventionally. It was a hot day. We were old enough to have small breasts. And suddenly, crashing out of the bush, a boy. Or was he a man? Alone, unshaven, pimpled, thick glasses. "Give me a kiss." I can't remember if he spoke English or French. And, stronger than we expected, he began to grab us and touch our breasts. His arms around our necks, we are locked in headlocks. "No," we demur. We are shocked but polite. We can't believe this is happening. I break away and begin walking. I look back and see the other Joanne struggling, but then she breaks away too and the boy—or was he a man?—retreats into the bush.

We keep walking and I don't remember whether we talked about what had just happened. I don't think we did. I know we didn't have to talk about whether to tell our parents. Of course, we wouldn't. All the gates would have come down, all the doors would have shut, all the keys would have turned in all the locks of all the glass coffins. Because we were girls. This is the bright red thread that runs through the fabric of my life, and the lives of so many girls, the never-ending struggle to hang on to rags and shreds of a freedom that is bought with silence and subterfuge.

But here's the thing I can't get over. I walked away. The other Joanne followed, soon enough, but I walked away. Would I have kept walking? Would I have turned back? That incident, so singular at the time, would of course repeat itself many times in many places: on the street, walking home at night, in any public space. Never really terrible, almost always banal. But that stab of self-knowledge—I walked away, and I'll never know if I would have turned back—was the beginning of something new and complicated.

# Elvira Madigan

IT OPENS WITH A YOUNG CHILD, A GIRL OF FIVE OR six, stooping, plucking, blowing the weightless silky seed fluffs of a milkweed plant. The child stops short, arrested by the sight of something nearby. Shot/reverse shot. Two bodies, a man and a woman, unmoving, entwined on the forest floor. A white parasol, a picnic basket. All so quick we can hardly take it in. The little girl turns and runs. High angle shot. The bodies below are motionless, all is still but for the humming and buzzing of insects. Suddenly the scene explodes with movement. Not dead, only asleep. The man's bottom has been stung by a bee and he reacts with hilarious, histrionic excess, rolling in the sunny grass, insisting he will never sit down again.

It is 1889. He is a Swedish cavalry officer, married with two children, who has deserted his post and his wife; she is a Danish tightrope walker who has run away from her stepfather's circus. In each other they have found themselves. They are playful, affectionate, tender, luminous with love. But as he shaves off his beard to disguise himself and turns to embrace her, the razor in his hand, its blade still heavy with shaving soap, rests against the back of her head, against the bare skin of her languid arm. They walk away and the sun shines through the fabric of her conventionally pretty butter-yellow dress, outlining her strong young legs. The second movement of Mozart's Piano Concerto No. 21 echoes throughout, plaintive, sweet, yearning.

I first saw *Elvira Madigan* almost fifty years ago when, several Saturdays in a row, a small handful of us—aged sixteen, I think—took the suburban commuter train into Montreal to attend a McGill student union international film series. We saw *The Loneliness of the Long Distance Runner*, Tony Richardson's bleak 1962 film based on the Alan Sillitoe short story of the same name. Black and white, British kitchen-sink realism, the angry working-class young man against the system. We saw Ingmar Bergman's 1957 film *The Seventh Seal*, brooding, impossibly confusing to my sixteen-year-old mind though the potent image of Death the chess player has stayed with me ever since. And we saw *Elvira Madigan*, the 1967 Swedish film directed by Bo Widerberg. Today the film is most remembered for its musical score, what the film credits describe as its "leitmotiv," Vivaldi's *Four Seasons* and, especially, the Andante from Mozart's Piano Concerto No. 21, which has, ever since then, been popularly known as the Elvira Madigan concerto. I remember being made breathless by the closing scene of the film, a freeze-frame shot of Hedvig, her face full of wonder, her hands raised to release the butterfly she has just caught, as two gunshots ring out. Oh! The unbearable sadness and beauty! The butterfly: her soul, their love!

Within six months of seeing that film my own first and overwhelming love showed up, a love that, like Hedvig's and Sixteen's, opened to the world of death, though less poignantly or picturesquely, or even mutually. Love and death, eros and thanatos. It would be corny if it wasn't so recurrently, insistently true, like a heartbeat. In the years that followed, I often thought I must have been primed, groomed for that first love by movies like *Elvira Madigan*, novels like *Wuthering Heights* ("It was not the thorn bending to the honeysuckles, but the honeysuckles embracing the thorn"), the inevitable *Romeo and Juliet* ("My bounty is as boundless as the sea, / My love as deep; the more I give to thee, / The more I have, for both are infinite"), even all the plaintive love songs of the era, from Percy Sledge's "When a Man Loves a Woman" to Marvin Gaye and Tammi Terrell's "Ain't No Mountain High Enough." Romantic love, that modern outgrowth of the medieval courtly love tradition, itself an outgrowth of the ancient blood sacrifice, Christ's endless and redeeming love. "Many waters cannot quench love, neither can the floods drown it." Perfect love. And could it even be love if it wasn't perfect, wasn't all-giving, all-embracing, all-forgiving.

At this great distance, it's difficult to remember all the details of my first love, my first lover. I remember him, of course, remember the thickness of his hair, the unfamiliar hardness of his body, his shoulders and arms and thighs, his cupid's bow mouth with its slightly overlapping front teeth. I remember his sensitivity. He took me to the art gallery; he loved the music of Jacques Brel; he wrote poetry. We skipped school and made out in the fields by the Back River—like Sixten and Hedvig! We walked in the rain. So far, so good. But he also told me that if my own poetry was published, it would only be to spite him, to say "I told you so." And, the most terrible thing of all, he wanted to die. He would say, "I'm going to do it tomorrow night" or next week or three days from now. I was terrified. My love was not enough. When he didn't phone

I went looking for him in the night, stumbling down the path toward the Back River, the crickets loud in my ears. When I was too frightened to go farther, I knew that I had failed him.

He didn't kill himself. His father found him a job at the Hudson's Bay store in Goose Bay, Labrador, where I visited him once, taking the small milk-run propeller plane that dropped down to several communities on its way from Montreal. At one of those stops, a man and his groomsmen got on board, the man dragging a fake ball and chain, on the way to his wedding in Goose Bay. I drank black coffee for the first time on that plane, and liked it. I had proper sex for the first time in Goose Bay. Of course, my parents did not want me to make that trip. As I write this, I remember that my father asked "Are you a virgin?" and I said "I don't know." I shouldn't have risked such an honest answer, an answer that made palpable the fumblings and misfires of teenage sex. It was an answer that drove my father crazy. It would be another handful of months before I disentangled myself from my first love. During that time, I telephoned him long distance, frequently, a very expensive thing to do; I gave him money; I listened. Once he told me a terrible story about one of his roommates in the Goose Bay boarding house, a young man who could not control his temper and threw his small dog against the wall. I have forgotten so much in my life, why can't I forget that story? Eventually something in me woke up—the "I am, I am" beat of my own heart in my own body. The relationship ended, though it wasn't the last time I loved beyond reason. What made me do it?

I go back to *Elvira Madigan* with that question in mind. I want to see again, but through the more knowing eyes of age, the fatal lure of romantic love, love beyond reason, the butterfly, the girl's soul, released into eternity, the freeze-frame image that has remained with me for more than half a century. I will see the film again and I will assess it coolly.

But the film is more delicate than I remembered and I have fallen in love, with it, all over again. Much has been written about the film's golden lushness. *TimeOut* dismisses it as a "candidate for the prettiest pic ever award." Roger Ebert calls it "remarkably beautiful," "alive and cinematic." But he also describes it as a film less about romantic love than about a kind of fatal "fanaticism," a tribute, he says, "to the human ego."

As I watch it now I am struck less by the film's visual beauty than by its soundtrack; the Mozart, yes, but also the Vivaldi, hurrying us from summer to fateful autumn. But even more than the music, it is the film's careful attention to all the quiet sounds that charms me and breaks my heart: the sounds of insects, of crickets, of birds, of dogs barking in the distance, of small bills and coins being counted, of chickens clucking, of wet clothes being shaken before they are hung up, of the wind in trees, of the wind in tall grass, of knitting needles, of feet walking on gravel or on cobblestones or on a leaf-strewn forest floor, of water lapping at the shore. Each sound clear and distinct, a thing—an ephemeral thing—in itself. And behind all of these sounds the inexorable march from summer to autumn, the knife cutting open the fish, the scythe in the field, the shaving blade against the neck, the spilled red wine staining the white cloth.

History haunts the film, but only a little. Hedvig, the tightrope walker, recounts a circus fire: "Our circus tent burned down in Paris. It was hit by a grenade. I was only two, but they told me all about it. It was '71. All our animals died in the fire. I can remember the smell." 1871, the Franco-Prussian War. And Sixten asks the fellow officer who tries to persuade him to return to his cavalry unit, "Do you know how many layers of skin a bayonet has to go through... before it reaches your guts?" But death doesn't need history; it doesn't require human intervention. Summer hastens toward autumn and every little thing dies. And so finally, for me, fifty years later, *Elvira Madigan* is a film about loving in the face of mortality, the mortality of the whole world, loving the whole world. Oddly, in the end, the suicides of Hedvig and Sixten, urged on by her and carried out by him, seem almost beside the point.

Maybe it's too late for me to examine my girl's heart, to answer the question that motivated me to watch *Elvira Madigan* once more. What made me do it? What made me love beyond reason? I only know that it was the mortal world, the beating of my own heart, the wind against my skin that brought me to my senses.

# The Italian Mechanic

I WAS NOT QUITE EIGHTEEN WHEN I STARTED work at the service desk of a Volkswagen dealership in Pointe Claire. The dealership was a short walk from Fairview Shopping Centre, the first fully enclosed shopping mall in all of Montreal, indeed in all of Quebec. At the time of its grand opening in 1965, my friends and I were at Girl Guide camp in the Laurentians, keenly aware of missing out on what we considered a major historical event. And perhaps it was, though not in the ways we imagined.

The first thing we did following release from our two-week sojourn in the wilderness was head to the mall. And what a mall it was. The apotheosis of its older sibling, the suburban strip mall, Fairview cradled us in air-conditioned or heated comfort. There was clean, highly polished flooring—if it wasn't marble, it might as well have been—and there were two large water fountains, one for each of the two retail anchors, Simpsons and Eaton's. Most astonishing of all, there was art: a fourteen-foot plaster replica of Michelangelo's David, purchased by Simpsons and gazing benignly into the air and past the rainfall water fountain in front of that department store. Notwithstanding its kitsch currency, its instant recognizability, it strikes me now as an odd choice. David, the young shepherd and slayer of giants, his slingshot hanging loosely over his left shoulder, his right hand cupping the fatal stone against his thigh. If he could gaze into the future, instead of past the water fountain, wouldn't he take his slingshot and blast a hole right in the middle of that Philistine mall, harbinger of the future and killer of neighbourhoods? Of course, he was also an odd choice for a Quebec smack in the middle of the Quiet Revolution, a Quebec that would eventually turn so many of its downtown churches *into* shopping malls. Whatever reasons Simpsons had for choosing David as their bid for high culture, he couldn't withstand the protests of suburban mothers unwilling to expose their children to his (relatively small) penis. He was gone within six months, banished to the Loyola College library where he would eventually watch over my studies before finally falling victim to a student prank twenty years later.

By the time I started work at the Volkswagen dealership, David had been gone a half-dozen years. At lunchtimes, I would walk the quarter mile from the dealership to the mall, and on paydays I would sometimes order a hot chicken sandwich from the lunch counter at the drug store: sliced chicken, white bread with the crusts cut off, french fries, canned peas, barbeque sauce gravy smothering everything. There was nowhere to eat at the dealership. Nowhere, that is, for the white- and pink-collar workers: the owners, the salespeople, a couple of office workers, and me. The mechanics all brought their lunch pails and ate near their workstations. Twice a day, for the morning and afternoon breaks, a small coffee truck would drive into the service garage, open its side panels, and dispense the chocolate bars and sweet cakes of the day, the

May Wests and "Joe Louies," along with the scalding hot coffee that tasted like pencil lead.

The dealership was a small and highly stratified world. There was the showroom, all plate glass and carpets and shiny new cars: the Squarebacks, the Fastbacks, the Beetles, the Karmann Ghias, the camper vans. This is where the owners lived, two brothers, both very short and unafraid of cutting the world down to their size, even literally. The younger brother, the vice-president, would invite visitors into his office, throw open his arms, gesturing to the child-size furniture, and say "Welcome to it's a small world!" The salespeople, who also lived in the plate glass region, ranged from the sleazy—the salesman who invited seventeen-year-old me to lunch on my first day of work and downed three martinis within the hour—to the sole saleswoman, ex-military, who gave me a kindly dressing down in the women's washroom as I wept there after being fired. I was a failed experiment.

The office, with its full-time secretary and part-time bookkeeper, came next, followed by the service division, a world within a world. Carl, the service manager, was German, a man with very short light brown hair and cheeks so closely shaven they were shiny. The assistant manager, Günter—also German, angular, dark-haired, tall, in wire-rimmed glasses—had a cubby in the body shop, a stand-up desk with a stool where he kept an eye on the work. The mechanics were all Italian or Caribbean, most of the Italians working in the body shop and most of the Caribbeans working on engines. There must have been regional differences that mattered a lot to them—what part of Italy, what island—but I was oblivious to them. Sandy-haired Dave, only slightly older than me, worked in the parts department. We were the only WASPS in our little cosmopolitan world, and this created a kind of unspoken fraternal agreement that we were not romantically interested in one another.

I was, of course, the only woman in the division, barely a woman, hired because the service manager thought a pretty face behind the counter was just the thing to assuage irate clients or attract new ones. He seemed genuinely indifferent to the fact that I didn't even have a driver's license, much less any clue about car repair. He had business cards made up for me: Jo-Ann Wallace, Service Advisor. I stood behind the counter and filled out requisition forms, describing symptoms: a shimmy in the steering wheel, squeaking brakes, malfunctioning windshield wipers. And then I walked the work orders through the shop, delivering them to Wolfgang in his cubby. Throughout my time there, which in the end was only five or six months, Michael Nesmith's song "Joanne" was on the hit parade, and it was often on the radio that played loudly in the shop all day long. Joanne, living in her meadow, driving around in desperation. The lyrics are a little enigmatic, and it is unclear who loves who more, or who leaves who in the end. The song followed me as I walked through the mechanical area into the body shop, in my dresses or my skirts, the owners having forbidden the women who worked for them from wearing pants in the workplace. I could hear the song above the drilling, the pounding, the hammering, the painting.

I was kindly treated. One of the Caribbean mechanics, Owen, would sometimes eat his lunch at the service counter, quietly, companionably, his face like a mask, saying nothing though I could feel desire washing off him. Günter willingly dealt with the nastier clients, leaning his loose frame against the counter, explaining the repair or the bill in his calm, methodical way. The easy, reserved camaraderie of a workplace that could have been very difficult for a young woman was broken only once, and then so gently it was hardly a ripple on the surface of our working lives.

One of the Italian mechanics had been away in Italy for about a month. He was a small, serious, compact man, probably in his late twenties, handsome, reticent, competent. On his return, he gave me a gift, a beautifully supple, dark blue, suede miniskirt wrapped in tissue paper. It was an extravagant gift and from a man with whom I had never exchanged more than a few words. I protested that I could not accept it, but he pointed out that he had also brought a gift for Carol, the office secretary. The suede of her skirt was not nearly so fine as that of mine. A few days later, he asked me out. No, I said, I have a boyfriend. This was more or less true, though the relationship was on its last legs. He didn't press me and I don't think we ever spoke again.

A short time later, one of the other Italian mechanics made his way to the service counter. He wanted me to know that his friend had been away in Italy to settle the estate of his uncle. As a beneficiary of the estate, he was now in a position to set up a home of his own, to find a wife and start a family. I think the friend told me this simply in explanation, but it was information I couldn't make sense of. I had plans. I read books, I wrote poetry, I knew I would go back to school. When he looked at me, what did the Italian mechanic see that would make him think I was wife material? That I could fit into his community, accommodate to him, to his family?

Even then I had an inkling that I had a face like a mirror. Maybe that's true of most very young women. But repeatedly over the next decade, strangers at bus stops or in convenience stores would speak to me in Italian or Portuguese or Yiddish. Once, at the bus stop at Bathurst and Eglinton in Toronto, an elderly woman with bad legs and a cane called me over.

Pressing money into my hand she asked me to go to a nearby store and buy bus tickets. When I came back with the tickets and her change, she took my hand in both of hers, searched my face, and said, in her heavily accented voice, "Thank you. You're a Jewish girl, aren't you?"

It is more than half a century later and my face, my face in public, is no longer a mirror. At most, it's a slight disruption in the field of vision, something like the ripple in the air above hot asphalt. Though it can be annoying to be always forgotten by people I've recently met or in shops I frequent, the truth is that I really don't mind at all. Looking out at the world when the world isn't looking back is liberating, absolving; it's a gift. And now, late in my life, I can finally look at the Italian mechanic—handsome, competent, dignified—without fear that my gaze will be construed as an invitation. And I just want to say, thank you. Thank you for accepting my inexperienced refusal with such quiet good grace.

# The Mercenary

THE LATE 1960S AND EARLY 1970S WERE MIGRATORY years for the baby boomers, hitchhiking back and forth across the country, scraping together the cash for a hippie camper van, taking to the air on youth standby tickets, filling up hostels everywhere. My own obligatory, if abbreviated, "Europe trip" happened in 1973 when I was twenty. It was only the second trip I'd ever taken in an airplane, the first being the flight to Labrador during which seventeen-year-old me discovered the sophisticated pleasure of black coffee.

My second adventure in air travel similarly required overcoming the objections of my parents—and especially the consistent, cold-shouldered maternal disapproval that shadowed my teenage and young adult years. Before I boarded the plane with my boyfriend, Richard, my aunt pulled me to one side and gave me some words of wisdom. Come back "as good" as you leave, she told me. By this she meant that I should come back a virgin, but that bird had already flown.

Richard and I had purchased the requisite army surplus rucksacks (olive drab canvas, heavy and awkward) together with lightweight, hostel-friendly sleeping bags, and booked our tickets to Brussels. Why Brussels? Only because landing there seemed more exotic and less predictable than landing in London or Paris, yet we could still make our way with what French we had. Being so little travelled, I found *everything* in Belgium exotic. The Grand-Place; the *Manneken Pis*; the pastries; the canals and cobbles of Bruges; the lace curtains in windows only inches from the sidewalks; Hieronymous Bosch's *Last Judgment*; the *steak américain* that surprised us by being steak tartar, not the hamburger steak we expected; the *café filtre*; the hostels, where I was kept awake by the snoring of German girls and dismayed by the damp white bread and huge vats of strawberry jam that constituted breakfast. Everything. All exotic.

And also terribly expensive. Within a week it became clear that we couldn't afford to stay on the Continent, and Richard suggested that, before we explore Britain, we crash with his cousins in England for a few days. Okay, I said. But we have to let them know we're coming. Give them a chance to invite us. No, no, said Richard. We'll just phone when we arrive at the train station in Nottingham. My pleas—for, *pace* my mother's disapproval, I was a polite young woman, sensitive to social norms—fell on Richard's amiably deaf ears. What was the problem? His cousins would be delighted to see us! And so, we boarded the ferry from Ostend to Dover and then the train to Nottingham.

We were in a small passenger compartment—so exotic! just like the movies! But I was weepy with frustrated embarrassment. And the only other person in the compartment was a middle-aged woman who stood for much of the trip, swaying with the movement of the train, her hand on the small of her back, reading from a book and laughing out loud—guffawing, really—at certain passages. It was already dark outside and we arrived in Nottingham very late at night. And of course, there was no answer when we telephoned Richard's cousins. The middle-aged woman was watching from the platform as I grew weepier. Come and stay with me, she said. You can phone your people in the morning. And Richard—ever amiable, ever willing to assume the best—accepted her invitation.

She was kindness itself. As we learned in the taxicab, she was on her way home from a Jehovah's Witness convention, standing on the train because of a bad back. She made up the guest room, pausing only at the end to ask: of course, you're married? Yes, said Richard, amiably. The next morning, she made us a full breakfast and café au lait, pouring the hot milk from a great height. She had learned this technique, she said, at one of her Jehovah's Witness conventions. Later, as we were getting ready to leave, she whispered to me: are you pregnant? sure that my weepiness must have been the consequence of hormones, and nothing so mundane as social embarrassment.

Richard's cousins greeted us without surprise and squeezed us in on a mattress somewhere in their cramped working-class flat in Nottingham. I remember so little of what happened next. A visit to the Major Oak in Sherwood Forest, purportedly the tree where Robin Hood hung out with his Merry Men. Thinking about D. H. Lawrence but not being able to connect what I was seeing with his novels. An evening at Ye Olde Trip to Jerusalem, one of a handful of pubs claiming to be the oldest in England, followed by a dance somewhere. But where?

A band was playing and we sat at tables in something like a community hall. A young man sat down and started chatting me up. He was a mercenary, he said, on his way to Northern Ireland. And then he asked me to dance. No! I said, appalled. And that really was the extent of my political engagement and political insight when I was in my twenties. Don't engage with the enemy and the enemy is anyone involved with the military or the police.

This put me in a bit of a pickle when we were moved along to stay with the next cousin. A bachelor, he lived in a small cottage on an estate in Thrumpton (a tiny village only a handful of miles southwest of Nottingham) where he worked as a kind of unofficial, part-time gamekeeper. But in his real job, his paying job, he was a narc—an undercover narcotics officer for the Nottingham police. In *his* cottage there was no nonsense about shared mattresses or shared guest rooms; I slept on a cot, a very slim fold-out cot, in the sitting room while Richard bunked down in the same room as his cousin. My aunt would have been pleased. This cousin was reserved, a little strict, maybe a bit put out by the way in which we disrupted the quiet country life he had built for himself outside of working hours. But in the mornings, he left fresh laid eggs on the counter for our breakfast, bits of feather and straw still sticking to them.

Richard's cousins always alluded to the estate as "the Byron estate." This thrilled me and I did my best to imagine the great poet striding through its copses and bits of forest. Wrong Byron, as I have only recently learned. It is Newstead Abbey, a good twenty miles north of Thrumpton, which was the poet's ancestral home, though it was in a state of near ruin when he inherited it and he never really lived there. Thrumpton Hall, on the other hand, was acquired by the son of a cousin of the poet, a full generation after the poet's death. It remained in that branch of the Byron family until 1949 when it passed along to George FitzRoy Seymour, a nephew by marriage of the childless Charlie Byron. So... wrong Byron and, by 1973, no Bryon at all. And yet, at the time of our visit, a quasi-Byronic drama was unfolding, full throttle, as it were, at the great house. In 2007 Miranda Seymour published a riveting, tell-all memoir of her father George's obsession, first with Thrumpton Hall and, in his middle- and late-middle age, with motorcycles, leathers, and a much younger and not quite literate working-class man.

I can be forgiven for not knowing anything about that, for not thinking to ask Richard's cousin, the narc, about Thrumpton Hall. But can I be so easily forgiven for not asking him much about himself? And why didn't I? Diffidence, inexperience, a sense perhaps that young women didn't speak frankly to men or express curiosity about their lives, the contradictions of their lives: loving the country, keeping chickens, busting drug dealers. This was the little bubble in which my young self travelled, at home and abroad, alert to so many small things and blind to so many big ones. Putting out my rudimentary antennae and waving them around a little, but then pulling them in too quickly, too soon. I would later learn that, at the time of our visit, the country cousin, the narc, was in love with the wife of the city cousin and had been for a long time. Eventually she would leave her husband for him and, astonishingly, they all remained friends.

And what of the mercenary? The young man about whom I remember nothing but a claim and an invitation: that he was a mercenary on his way to Northern Ireland and that he asked me to dance. I look but find no evidence that the British employed mercenaries in Northern Ireland. And only now does it occur to me that the claim might have been nothing more than a young man's misguided attempt to impress a very young woman.

# Carole with an E

WE MET IN MR. ISMAEL'S HIGH SCHOOL GEOMETRY class, both of us sitting at the back of the room. Mr. Ismael was, in the context of our academically uninspired school, an uncommonly good teacher, calm and respectful. There were times in his classroom when I almost, almost intuited the lyrical beauty at the heart of geometry. But high school was not the right time for me to learn science or math, at least not as it was taught then. In her 1952 novel, *Martha Quest*, Doris Lessing describes sixteen-year-old Martha as "turned in on herself, in a heavy trancelike state." She feels "dragged," "weighted," as if she were "acting against... her intellect." That was, in many ways, my experience of the teenage years. Maybe it was hormonal. Whatever the cause, a lot of school stuff just wasn't sticking. I had a Teflon brain. Even our home economics teacher, normally the kindest and most patient of women, was driven to distraction by my inability to retain, from one week to the next, any memory of how to thread a sewing machine. "Jo-Ann," she finally burst out, almost certainly shocking herself, "you're so stupid!"

I was and I wasn't. Simmering under that non-stick

surface was a growing sense of how I wanted to live, what I wanted to learn, who I wanted to be. In Carole I found what L. M. Montgomery's Anne of Green Gables—Anne with an e—would have called a kindred spirit. We bonded initially by discovering that we both had a crush on the same Bee Gee: Robin, the homely one. It would have been too easy to have a crush on Barry, the eldest, the smoothly handsome one with great hair, or Maurice, Robin's fraternal twin, who compensated for his already receding hairline with shimmery confidence and blandly symmetrical features. Robin, alone of the three, was truly homely: a large gap-toothed overbite; sad, droopy, pouched eyes; unfortunate hair. Even as a very young man, his whole face appeared to be dragged down by small invisible weights. These were the pre-disco, pre-*Saturday Night Fever* Bee Gees, the Bee Gees of ballads like "To Love Somebody" and "Words" and "I Started a Joke." Choosing the homely Bee Gee as our favourite (you always had to have a favourite) was a mark of our own complicated, artistic sensibilities, our yearning, dreaming souls.

And Carole Strypchuk, Carole with an e, was big souled. Big souled in a tiny body. Not quite five feet tall, she was a little squat, almost dwarfish. She was flat chested with a round Slavic face, very thin blonde hair, vivid and uncompromising blue eyes, and a beautifully deep, expressive voice. After all, as she frequently claimed, she was named after Carole Lombard. Carole with an e. She also claimed that her mother was William Shatner's cousin. And that her father's family was White Russian. I had no idea what this meant but I imagined unhappy bejeweled political refugees in heavily draped rooms, remembering the old country.

Of course, her family life was nothing like that. Our high school was a large, new, composite suburban school that drew its student body from the largely Anglophone towns of Dollard-des-Ormeaux, Roxboro, and Pierrefonds. Carole, together with her younger sister and brother, lived in a split-level house in Pierrefonds. They had a squat yellow dog that loved being scratched at the base of its tail. Mr. Strypchuk, who could have been Edward G. Robinson's twin brother, did have a kind of brooding White Russian intensity. Mrs. Strypchuk mostly sat benignly at the kitchen table, smiling abstractedly and smoking. During my visits to their home, Carole and I would retreat to the basement rec room where we would compose show tune parodies, none of which I can remember. Or we would design the coffee house we planned to open. We might visit Carole's younger sister, Gail, in her room to have our horoscopes charted. But there were a couple of visits when Mrs. Strypchuk, normally so placid, would answer the door and hiss angrily, "She thinks she's so great! But she's not!" before being pushed aside by Carole, who would peep out, "Not a good time," and then close the door in my face.

What Carole and I shared most was longing for an artistic, a bohemian life. And we were determined to make a head start on it. We took the commuter train into Montreal and ate at Pam Pam, the Hungarian restaurant cum coffee shop on Stanley Street, where I had dumplings for the first time, with some kind of paprika sauce. Another time we met just after dawn on a late spring morning, to take bennies, Benzedrine, before hopping the earliest train and heading to Old Montreal where we used my father's 8 mm home movie camera to film winos lurching down the filthy streets. We persuaded ourselves we were high. We later intercut these scenes with filmed images of garbage cans and tomato soup cans, and called our little film *Andy Warhol: Eat Your Heart Out*. When I got a driver's license and could borrow my mother's car, we would drive out to Dorval airport (now the Pierre Elliott Trudeau International Airport), buy a drink in the dimly lit bar, and pretend we were waiting for our flight to Paris. Sometimes I would drive home from Carole's at night, playing the radio, with the smell of the Back River coming through the wide-open windows of the car, and I would wonder: When does it start? My real life?

But Carole's real life, her artistic life, started early and auspiciously. In grade nine or ten she was accepted to a weekend program at the National Theatre School where Maurice Podbrey was assistant director of the English section. This was around the time that he founded the Centaur Theatre, and in Centaur's inaugural year, 1969, Carole made her professional debut in the role of Mary McGregor in *The Prime of Miss Jean Brodie*. I sat with two or three friends in the darkened playhouse in the Old Montreal Stock Exchange Building, my very first experience of live theatre, and I was astonished: the proximity, the "making do" of small companies without elaborate sets, the risk.

I have a photo of Carole taken only a year or two later when we were both at Vanier College, one of the province's earliest Anglophone CEGEPs. The college had opened only a couple of months earlier, occupying the buildings that once housed the convent and school of the Soeurs de Sainte-Croix. It was now a place of exuberant anarchy, staffed by newly minted PhD draft dodgers and hippies. We pulled our final grades out of a hat, Dada-like, or we shared them on good Marxist principles: from each according to his abilities, to each according to his needs. If you planned to go on to medical school, you needed a higher grade; if you planned to go on unemployment insurance (as it was called then) for a while, a lower grade would suffice. We wandered the buildings where small pockets of nuns were still packing and moving; we climbed the unsecured bell tower in the chapel that became our library, smoked joints in small forgotten rooms, hung out in the cemetery. That is where I took Carole's photo, later developing it in the college darkroom. She sits on a snowy set of stairs, wearing a small hand-knitted shawl, blue jeans, and suede boots. She looks back over her shoulder and up at me as I stand above her; she looks serious and vulnerable, though this may be an effect of time. We look at each other across the years and I have to remind myself that I am now older than her mother was then. Older than any of her teachers. Older than she will ever be.

Following CEGEP Carole secured a couple of roles in small, alternative productions in Montreal before moving to Toronto to really launch her theatrical career. She got an agent and sent me copies of the photos in her acting portfolio. She is gamine-like, with a French sailor's striped top and beret. She is tinier than ever because she cannot afford to eat properly. She has a small room in a kind of boarding house on Sherbourne Street where the occupants are all aspiring artists—directors, drummers, actors—and she is in love with Marcel. "Do you know," she writes to me, "that I have never slept with anyone with brown eyes before?" She misses Montreal. She has terrible dreams that her mother has died. Some months later she seems to have found herself in a sort of brief ménage à trois with a couple in the house. She tries cocaine, I don't know how often. On one occasion I visit her in the rooming house on Sherbourne Street. She leans over and rubs my breasts, a little experimentally, which surprises me. The gesture feels more business-like than erotic, and neither of us says anything about it.

Finally, the big break arrives: the 1977 premiere of Carol Bolt's *One Night Stand* at the Tarragon Theatre. It is an excellent theatre and a strong cast: Brent Carver plays Rafe and Chapelle Jaffe plays Daisy; Carole plays... the dead body. For most of the second act she is stuffed behind pillows on the bed, only to be pulled out at the play's climactic moment. As Carole described it in a letter to me: "I lay sprawled across the bed, my eyes open, facing the audience while mayhem broke loose about me." The play is a huge success and Bolt is immediately commissioned to write a film adaptation. The two principle actors are invited to appear in the film; Carole is not. For another handful of years, she continued to cobble together a life in the theatre, mostly by working as a property mistress, always hand to mouth, always happy to receive small gifts of food or cigarettes, or to be invited for a meal.

And here is where I begin to lose my way, because we begin to drift apart. It's like I'm reading a book consisting of chapter titles followed by blank pages. Carole Gives Up the Theatre and Goes Back to School. Something Happens to Carole's Mother. Carole's Father Dies. Carole Moves Back to the Family Home in Pierrefonds to Care for Her Brother and Sister. And of course, Carole's brother and sister need care because they have inherited their mother's bipolar disorder, or something like it. I hear about Carole now and then because—needing the money, but needing the company even more—she sometimes takes the train into Montreal to work a few hours in a vintage clothing boutique owned by mutual friends.

It is painful to reread Carole's letters now, the ones she sent during her first two years in Toronto, full of her dreams but full also of love: for me, for her sister and mother. I wish I could remember when I last saw her. It might have been the time that I visited Montreal and a group of us—my oldest friend Gaby, my sister Catherine, her oldest friend Joan, Carole, and I—went out to dinner at a restaurant in the west end neighbourhood of Notre-Dame-de-Grâce. We ended up downtown and then at a Metro station, Gaby and I on one side, heading west, Carole on the other side, heading east to catch the commuter train back to Pierrefonds. We are laughing and calling to one another across the tracks. The camera pulls away and the credits come up.

Some years later Carole died quite suddenly at fifty, only a few days after complaining of a headache. A friend who was at the funeral said it was sparsely attended. Carole's brother and sister seemed a bit dissociative and apparently unconcerned about their own future.

When I taught myself to knit, one of the of the first things I made, in memory of Carole, was a little totemic pouch. I hung it on a bulletin board in my home office, but now it lives in a small basket made of sweetgrass, a gift from Carole. I pull the basket off the bookshelf beside my desk and take out the knitted pouch. It is sewn shut, decorated with a couple of purple ribbons, a tiny silver owl pin (another gift from Carole), and three bird feathers. The pouch is stuffed with cotton batting, but I can feel something inside it. What did I put in there, before sewing it shut? What is that tiny, hard thing that must, at one time, have been emblematic of our friendship? It strikes me that this is how memory works, through a process of conscious and semi-conscious accretion, the original seed now only barely discernible.

# Uncle Joe

WHEN I WAS LITTLE, I THOUGHT MY UNCLE JOE was the most glamorous person I knew. "My uncle is a playboy," I proclaimed proudly to my schoolmates. How did I come up with such a locution? Playboys were in the air. Hugh Hefner's first TV show, *Playboy's Penthouse*, had aired just a couple of years earlier and of course the magazine, with its aura of casual and progressive sophistication, was everywhere. Hefner described his show as "a sophisticated weekly get together of people that we dig and who dig us." I dug my uncle.

In *A Child's Christmas in Wales*, Dylan Thomas says, "There were always Uncles at Christmas," and certainly I had my share of them. Uncle Wesley, who was married to my mother's oldest sister, and who always called my mother Gracie because she reminded him of a former girlfriend. Wesley was a welder, bony-faced and kind, with a soft spot for children and a steel plate in his head because he had been injured while training for the Second World War. The injury kept him from the front. There was Uncle Jim, who was married to my mother's other sister. It was understood that we didn't talk about Jim who, it was also understood but not spoken of, was both deranged and violent. He eventually died alone in a cabin in rural Quebec and his body was discovered only when a neighbour became aware of the stench two weeks later. My aunt's sons had, years earlier, staged an intervention and spirited their mother and her broken wrist away to Alberta where she joined the Salvation Army church. She insisted on being buried with Jim upon her own death. At the other end of the spectrum, there was Uncle Harold who was married to my father's sister. Reserved and soft-spoken, Harold had somehow, inexplicably, started off as a Pentecostal minister before eventually becoming a Methodist. It must have been a great relief to him to no longer have to speak in tongues and roll in the aisles. Uncle Bruce was my father's younger brother. Handsome and charming, he hightailed it to Detroit at a young age to work his way up in the automobile industry, persisting in a mild flirtation with my mother on his rare and sentimental trips home to Montreal.

And then there was Joe, my father's older brother. A snappy dresser, there was something in his manner of speaking, a kind of faux American flatness, that evoked movie actors of the 1940s. He was very much a product of that decade and the early 1950s, a time when Montreal was a wide-open city, famous for its red-light district, its gangsters, its nightclubs. The El Morocco, the Bellevue Casino, the Copacabana. The kinds of places where the tips were so good that waiters, like Joe, signed their paycheques back to the bosses, a requirement of working there. Joe had already inherited a taste for the good life and fast money from his father, Bob, who left his job at the Coca Cola plant to set up as a bookmaker in 1941. When I was a teenager, meeting my dates at some halfway point, my mother would object, "Your father always picked me up at my door." I later learned that, not only did my mother make her own way by streetcar to the Christophe-Colomb Avenue apartment of her future in-laws, but she stopped at the corner store to pick up the racing sheets for Bob. Of course, all this happened before I was born. In 1954, the year following my birth, Jean Drapeau was elected mayor and, together with the evocatively named interim police chief, Pacifique Plante, embarked on a morality crusade, a thirty-year campaign to clean up the city.

It's unclear to me how Joe earned his living during those years, and it's possible he didn't. He would show up at our apartment, and later at our new house in the suburbs, usually at Christmastime and always with a beautiful woman on his arm. At least, the women seemed very beautiful to me. Carefully made up, their hair fashionably bouffant, young and eager to please, they were introduced as "hostesses." Air hostesses? Restaurant hostesses? Who knew. Upon arrival, Uncle Joe would examine our fingernails, the fingernails of four little girls, which of course were never spotless. My mother remembers this with irritation. One Christmas he arrived with gifts. The tag on mine read "To Jo from Joe," and the promisingly small box contained a necklace and screw back earrings set with black stones, certainly paste jewelry though I persisted in calling them black diamonds. Maybe they were. Maybe they fell off the back of a truck. I was around eleven years old and my mother was furious. "Joe," she said, "that's no gift for a child."

"To Jo from Joe." The thrill of the acknowledgement, the feeling of being picked out, being special. The feeling especially sharp because of the memory of an incident a year or two earlier. We were at the beach and Uncle Joe was there with a beautiful woman. They were making a fuss of my youngest sister who was about two years old and who I adored. I knew that by playing with the adorable toddler the woman was trying to communicate something to my uncle. But I also knew, with a sinking certainty, that I had passed some kind of best-before date. Despite my determined efforts, I could not attract their attention. I was no longer cute, not yet pretty.

Shortly after the black diamond Christmas my uncle stopped coming to the house. "Where's Uncle Joe?" I would ask. "He's in the United States," my parents would answer. The United States? In fact, he was only a couple of short kilometres away from where we used to live in our upper duplex in Montreal north. The black flag that Bordeaux Prison raised following an execution was visible from our back balcony, the last hanging at that jail taking place in 1960. Of course, Joe was not hanged. He was in for passing a bad cheque.

I was middle-aged by the time the story came out. My father at work and all the kids at school, my mother was home alone when there was pounding at the door and a handful of police officers burst in. "Where is he? Where is he?" Yelling mostly in French, going room to room, kicking the dog, a cocker spaniel, because it wouldn't stop barking. My mother tears up as she recalls this detail. She telephoned my father who had taken the commuter train downtown and felt very far away. She was terrified but also anxious about what the neighbours in this new suburb would think. They phone afterwards to see if she is okay. Why did Joe use our address?

It is years before Joe is admitted back into our lives, still the same smooth talker and still with a beautiful woman on his arm. But Pauline, though glamorous, is not young and she has had a life of her own. She is, in fact, slightly terrifying in the way of determinedly glamorous women, her makeup, the alarming hair, the masses of jewelry giving her a scarily shellacked quality. I am tongue-tied in her presence but, to my surprise, my parents are crazy about her. She is certainly the life of the party, on one occasion removing quiet Uncle Harold's shoes and giving him a salacious foot massage. Harold cannot stop giggling.

No longer the big city swell, Joe was living at Pauline's house in Owen Sound when he died of prostate cancer, the same disease that killed his father. We all drove down for the funeral. Pauline's daughters—blonde, tanned, beautifully dressed and made-up—were there. We were at the funeral home visitation when a pair of stiletto heels made their way down the staircase and Pauline's voice rang out, "Why so quiet? Anyone would think there's a funeral going on!"

Years and years later I am leaving work, and as I head to the elevator, one of my male colleagues, normally the kindest and gentlest of men, slams down his phone. "Fuck," he yells, "fuck, fuck, fuck." I gasp in alarm and turn to flee when he sees me and is ashamed, conciliatory. But that night I have a terrible nightmare, the theme of which is "big Joe is beating little Jo," pummeling, pounding, the two figures blobby and inchoate. Or, for my sense of the meaning is only audible not visual, is it "big Jo is beating little Jo"? What is it about the experience of what felt like violent male anger that prompted this dream? Although it makes me uncomfortable, I can't turn away from acknowledging that the image in my dream is clearly masturbatory, male masturbatory. While I don't remember ever witnessing a man exposing himself or masturbating himself, that doesn't mean it didn't happen. Any sexual assaults that I do recall were by strangers; they were all relatively minor, stopping well short of violence and never getting very far. Just the usual crap: a stranger trying to grab my breast as he passed in the street, a wedding guest pinning me up against a post ("Have you ever kissed a black man before?"), a young man trapping me in the revolving door of the downtown Eaton's. My mother was uncomfortable with what she saw as Uncle Joe's sexualization of me when he gave me screw-on earrings for Christmas. I am more inclined to think of the earrings as a lazy, thoughtless gift, something he had on hand that could have been given to any one of a number of… I was going to write "girls or women," but of course it really was an inappropriate gift for a young girl. If anything ever happened with Uncle Joe, it is locked away in some Bordeaux Prison of my mind. After all, a single enigmatic dream by a woman in her middle age is not evidence of anything.

# North American Factors

I HATED HIGH SCHOOL SO MUCH THAT, WHEN I graduated, the first thing I did was throw out all my yearbooks. I didn't want to risk turning those pages, seeing those faces, and, in later years, feeling sentimental about the whole thing. As I saw it, our new comprehensive high school was in the business of making us stupider. There was the math and phys. ed. teacher, Mr. Barnes, who peered down the tops of the girls in his classes, often dropping a piece of chalk in front of them so they would bend over to pick it up. The English teacher, Mr. Rosenbaum, who loved trading quips with the cool boys and telling us about how he had gone to McGill with Leonard Cohen. When he was unprepared for class, he would give us a free period in which to do our homework, but he forbade us from reading non-homework books. Our chemistry teacher Mr. Schuman. Finding him incomprehensible, I failed the first term and only passed the course by teaching myself sufficient introductory chemistry from my father's old textbook. The very young North American literature teacher who tried harder than anyone to connect with us, giving us mimeographed Bob Dylan and Simon &

Garfunkel lyrics to study as poetry. She was thin and nervous and wore thick woolen suits, almost certainly in order to add a little heft to her tiny frame. She didn't last very long before collapsing in tears in the middle of a class and disappearing forever.

The progressive or free school movement was all the rage then, and I *begged* my parents to send me to one. I had read A. S. Neill's *Summerhill*, based on his famous English coeducational boarding school. Summerhill's educational philosophy emphasized the innate goodness of children, and its basic tenets were freedom and equality. Students took classes or not, as they pleased and when they pleased. I knew that I was hungry for knowledge, and I also knew that I wasn't getting it in any meaningful way. Or at least not in a way that worked for me. I did my best to build up my own little library with books like Louis Untermeyer's *A Concise Treasury of Great Poems*, but I had so little guidance.

Unsurprisingly, my parents had never heard such nonsense. They were unwilling to pay for piano lessons, never mind a free school. Our discussion probably lasted no more than five minutes. But I wasn't on my own. In 1968, the Hall-Dennis Report on "the aims and objectives of education in the schools of Ontario" was published. It was highly critical of the state of public schooling, which it described as "imposed, involuntary, structured. The pupil becomes a captive... from the day of entry." Among other things, it recommended the elimination of "lock-step systems of organizing pupils, such as grades, streams, programs, etc.," "freeing children to engage any subject on any level where it interested them." Our firebrand high school student union president held a day-long retreat on the free school movement, and we agitated for change. Here is the change we got: a smoking pit was set up outside the school cafeteria so that students, like teachers, could smoke on school grounds.

I carried my animus about schooling into CEGEP, which was a little ironic because the anarchic disorganization of Vanier College in its first year of operation made it effectively a free school. And there were aspects of it that I loved. A janitor's room that a small group of us, from all over the city, took over, making it our own, establishing a little community. The smell of toast on rainy mornings in the cafeteria. The library, as it took shape in the former chapel. Regardless, I quit before the end of the first semester. My parents were furious. Although I insisted that I would eventually go back to school, they felt that I was throwing away opportunities that had never been theirs.

It was an especially bitter pill for my father to swallow. He had been accepted at McGill University when he graduated from high school, but he took night courses at Sir George Williams University (now Concordia) instead. I had always assumed that he couldn't afford the tuition, couldn't afford not to work full-time. And I'm sure that's true. But a few years ago, one of my sisters told me something that fleshes out this period of his life in a poignant way. My father asked his mother to buy him a wardrobe that would be suitable for McGill and, when she refused—she was, after all, working as a waitress—he opted for night school. And never really forgave his mother. To me, this little vignette opens up a whole world. On the one hand, it is very characteristic of my father, who really did believe that clothes make the man. He began to wear bespoke tailored suits long before he could afford them. His dress shirts always went to the dry cleaner where he insisted that the cuffs be starched, but not the collar. Every night he shone his shoes and pressed the crease back into his trousers, using a handkerchief to protect the woolen fabric from getting shiny. Even at home, you could never describe his outfits as relaxed. But I also think his deeply felt need for an appropriate university wardrobe says something about a fantasy of college life. I was not immune to this fantasy. Even before I went back to school, I pored over the "college" issues of *Mademoiselle* and *Glamour* magazines. Theirs was a world of perpetual red-and-gold autumn; a world of tartans and woolens and just the right coat, of bright smiles and books clasped in arms. It was not a fantasy of the life of the mind; it was, instead, a fantasy of belonging.

And clearly, I was refusing to belong. My parents laid out the new ground rules. I would have to get a job immediately, before the second term began, and I would have to pay room and board. The part they didn't tell me was that they would basically refuse to talk to me for almost two years. I was seventeen years old.

So, I found work. My first job was at a clothing factory where I was one of four women who printed the little tags that told the piecework machinists what to do with their bits of cloth. At the factory, we all punched in and out at a time clock, starting work at 8:00 in the morning and finishing at 5:30 in the afternoon with two fifteen-minute coffee breaks and a half hour for lunch. We worked Saturday mornings. It goes without saying that the factory was not unionized, but we seem not to have been protected even by ordinary labour law. When, a year or two earlier, the union had tried to organize the factory, the owners gave the workers a five-cent-an-hour raise and that was enough to buy them off. The women I worked with, all Italian, couldn't figure out whether I was a management spy or a union mole looking for the next opportunity. Either way, they didn't trust me. I lasted two months.

My Volkswagen job was next, followed by a job in the stock-room of a discount department store, putting price tags on things. It was filthy work, and I was always covered in dust and ink, my fingernails and cuticles torn from opening boxes.

The job at North American Factors was the last one I held before going back to school. The whole time I worked there, probably six or seven months, I had no idea what a factoring company does. While the process still seems a little opaque to me, the gist of it, in the words of Investopedia, is this: "A factor is essentially a funding source that agrees to pay a company the value of an invoice less a discount for commission and fees." The factoring company then collects on those invoices. The advantage to the business, often a business whose customers typically take longer to pay, is that it frees up cash flow. It was only much later, when I moved out West, where so much of the land claimed by settlers effectively traces the movements of the Hudson's Bay Company, that the word *factor* would resonate in different ways. The factor was the man in charge of an HBC post. They were frequently well po-sitioned to claim the best farmland in the surrounding area.

I got the job at North American Factors through a friend, someone who was a member of our little janitor's room gang, whose father was the firm's chief accountant and office man-ager. Like me, Dafna had left CEGEP long before completing the two-year program; unlike me, she acquired a glossy sur-face and a professional wardrobe and now worked as secre-tary to the president. I was hired as a filing clerk.

All the principals in the firm, including my friend Dafna and her father, were Jewish; most of the office staff were not. We were all, I think, Anglophone. The business was housed in a nine- or ten-storey office building on Bleury just below St. Catherine. The building was a pretty non-descript example of the International Style, all straight angles and glass and concrete, and most of the other tenants were in the needle trade, then a major industry in Montreal. There was a small greasy spoon restaurant on the ground floor and an excellent magazine store at the corner of Bleury and St. Catherine. North American Factors employed somewhere around twenty-five people: a receptionist, a mail boy, a couple of filing clerks, a handful of accounting clerks—who spent their time at adding machines, adding up invoices and then adding them up again—and typists and secretaries and a couple of low-level managers. The executive suite, where Dafna worked, was separate from the main office, carpeted and hushed.

But our corner—bright and noisy with linoleum flooring and typewriters and adding machines and mail carts—was full of human drama, full of character and narrative, full of women's stories. Almost half a century later, I remember with uncanny vividness the faces of my co-workers. There was Maeve, a filing clerk and fill-in receptionist. Strawberry blonde, a real potty mouth, she looked a little worn and older than her age, which was close to mine. Maeve had a little boy, a toddler, who she loved fiercely but mostly secretly because he was illegitimate, something about which her Irish Catholic family felt deeply. I remember the day she screwed up her courage to tell our boss, Dafna's father, that she had a child. He was a serious, worried man who received the news kindly but probably also with some bemusement. Why should it matter to him or to North American Factors that Maeve had a child?

There was Nina, the receptionist. Dark haired, dark eyed, she was smudgy, not unattractive but always a little unkempt and just a little... not quite clean. Like Maeve, she was around my age, large breasted, slightly pot-bellied, her clothes always a little florid and ill fitting. She wore platform shoes and seemed unsteady on her feet. One day she asked me to repair the split crotch seam of her velveteen pants while she sat on the toilet in the women's washroom. The pants were... not quite clean. Another day she told me about giving Saul, the president's brother, a blow job in his office in exchange for a new sweater. Saul, the handsome but feckless younger brother, married, was a small-scale clothing distributor and he had office space in North American Factors on sufferance. Nina reported the incident matter-of-factly and clearly regarded it as a fair exchange. Her mother was severely asthmatic and Nina, their financial mainstay, telephoned her several times a day.

Now and then Maeve, Nina, one of the accounting clerks, and I would head downstairs to the greasy spoon for our morning coffee break. The accounting clerk would order two fried eggs which she cut delicately into ribbons before eating them. I don't know why this made such an impression on me. Maybe it's because, unlike Maeve and Nina, she was precise and reserved and so her smallest actions carried a mysterious weight.

Is it odd that I remember less about myself and what I was like back then, back there, in that building on Bleury below St. Catherine, than I do about them? I can't remember if my hair was long or short, what I wore, whether I brought my lunch to work with me. I must have taken the commuter train in from my parents' house in the suburbs and then walked the seven or eight blocks from Central Station to Bleury. I must have done that, but I don't remember it.

I do remember leaving the building on my lunch hours and walking, walking, walking. Sometimes I would walk the half dozen blocks to Phantasmagoria Records on Park

Avenue, which is what Bleury turns into north of Sherbrooke. Phantasmagoria was my id, my dream life, wild, untrammelled. A late-Victorian storefront, its windows painted in innocent back-to-the-garden psychedelic hopefulness, its walls lined with album covers, most of its floor occupied by old velvet couches and a massive aquarium, the air always heavy with the smell of cigarettes and joints and incense. I was a filing clerk who took the commuter train in from the suburbs. I didn't belong there, but, oh, how I wanted to.

When I didn't walk to Phantasmagoria Records, I might walk the dozen blocks to the Classic Book Shop on St. Catherine Street near de la Montagne. Or if it was raining, I might simply walk to the corner and browse in the magazine store. That is where, in spring 1972, I bought the preview issue of *Ms. Magazine* with its bright red cover: its eight-armed, blue-skinned goddess Kali, tears pouring down her cheeks as she balances a mirror, an iron, a typewriter, a frying pan, a little haloed saviour baby in her belly. The magazine pointed to me and called my name; it jumped right off the magazine rack and into my hands. I had already read Simone de Beauvoir's *The Second Sex* and Germaine Greer's *The Female Eunuch*, its then shocking cover image—the hanging, handled flesh corset—an exhilarating kick in the gut. I was reading Doris Lessing. I was reading the early Margaret Drabble, Margaret Atwood, Marie-Claire Blais, Sylvia Plath. Bit by bit I was putting a world together, a world that had people like me at the centre: young women feeling something, wanting something, just about bursting with something.

And here's where Ricky Rubenstein comes into things, but only briefly. Ricky Rubenstein, recently back from a few months on an Israeli kibbutz and earning some money at North American Factors before, like me, heading back to school in the fall. Bearded, brown-eyed, smart, a little confrontational, an intellectual equal. We shared books, including *The Female Eunuch*. We made out at a party at Dafna's house. I should feel ashamed or embarrassed as I write this; after all, I was almost nineteen, too old for that kind of behaviour. Instead, I feel amused, glad that I behaved a little badly, glad that he was a good kisser, glad of his slightly soft and comfortable body. Later we met for coffee at the McGill Student Union, and it was pretty clear the relationship wasn't going anywhere. He was still full of the kibbutz and a shiksa was not how he imagined his future. That was fine with me.

In retrospect, it interests me that he was at McGill, and I was starting over again at CEGEP. Like my father, I had my own fantasy of university life and, instead of heading back to Vanier College, I opted to attend Marianopolis College, a small, private CEGEP in a beautiful old building in Westmount. I imagined it would be a cut above. Founded in 1908 by a Catholic women's congregation, I soon discovered that it was too conservative and, in a way, too incurious for my needs. I lasted only one semester before transferring back to Vanier. But Marianopolis did give me something unpredictable, a kind of gift. The school's library was wood panelled, beautiful, and completely disorganized. It had a fireplace. At the time, I was in love with the idea of the Cuban Revolution, and I was writing an essay about it. Stuffed away at the bottom of a set of library shelves, I discovered a stack of old *Maclean's* magazines from the 1950s, and suddenly I was *there*, in real time, following events as they unfolded. My essay sprang to life. I even dreamed about the Cuban Revolution at night. A stack of old magazines in an inadequate library in a beautiful building—an incongruous set of factors—showed me what real learning was like.

I still think about Maeve and Nina and their messy, loving lives. I think about the factors that conspire to enable some of us to escape.

# Whimsy

Last night I saw upon the stair,
A little man who wasn't there
He wasn't there again today
Oh, how I wish he'd go away...

William Hughes Mearns, from "Antigonish," 1899

ONE OF MY EARLIEST MEMORIES IS OF LYING
awake in the bedroom I shared with my sister Nancy and listening to the television in the next room. It's possible that I
snuck out of the bedroom and crouched in the hallway, peeking around the corner. It wouldn't have been the first time.

My parents were watching the 1950 movie *Harvey*, starring Jimmy Stewart. Stewart plays Elwood P. Dowd, a forty-two-year-old man whose best friend is an imaginary six-foot,
three-and-a-half-inch rabbit named Harvey. Elwood, who
is financially well off and apparently unemployed, likes his
martinis. He frequents unassuming bars where he is unfailingly polite, both to the patrons, some of whom are clearly
indigent, and to Harvey, always inviting the rabbit to go first
through a doorway and ensuring that he has the most comfortable seat. Elwood's older sister Veta has come to live with
him following the death of their mother and she is anxious
to marry off her gangly daughter Myrtle Mae. But the tea
parties Veta arranges for the mothers of suitable young men
are invariably ruined when Elwood shows up and insists on
introducing the ladies to Harvey. Veta decides she must have

Elwood committed to Chumley's Rest Home, a sanitorium. Mayhem ensues when she confesses to the house psychiatrist that "Every once in a while, I see this big white rabbit myself. Now isn't that terrible? What's more, he's every bit as big as Elwood says he is." "Sound the gong," says the psychiatrist, "We mustn't let that woman leave the grounds." And so, while Elwood wanders away to pick flowers in the sanitorium garden, his sister Veta is the one who is committed. The usual shenanigans prevail and the movie concludes when the owner and operator of the rest home, Dr. Chumley, asks Elwood if Harvey could please stay with him. Elwood, ever accommodating, sadly agrees. But, at the last minute, Harvey changes his mind and leaves with Elwood.

I wish I could remember how old I was when I overheard this movie. What I do know is that it made a huge impression on me and was doubtless at least partially responsible for me acquiring my own invisible friend. In my case, it was an invisible dog, a Scottish terrier named, inevitably, Scotty. My dog Scotty didn't hang around the house much but he was always there on family outings, trotting along amiably at the end of his leash. I don't think I ever told my parents or sisters about him, not out of a sense of shame but because he was *my* dog.

I don't know when Scotty faded away, like Puff, the magic dragon, but it was before we acquired our first real dog when I was ten, a blond American cocker spaniel. He was named, inevitably, Scamp, after the Disney comics character. The white leatherette diary I kept when I was eleven—a gift, complete with a little lock and key—includes the following entry: "I went to the store this morning with Scamp. I bought some chips and shared them with Scamp. When we got home Scamp had to go into the basement because his paws were wet. I went with him and had a game of ball with him." A few days later I recorded that "I took Scamp to the store and we got ourselves a small bag of candy." Scamp was killed by a neighbour's car when I was sixteen, my first experience of devastating, almost incomprehensible, loss.

I certainly wasn't alone in having an imaginary friend. Research suggests that somewhere around sixty-five percent of children create them and that it is a normal part of childhood development. My oldest friend Gaby was among the minority of kids who never had an imaginary friend. We met when we were nine years old, our families moving at the same time into the same suburban development. Her house was directly across the street from mine and the empty lots, the half-built houses, the as yet unpaved streets, the mud, the bulldozers and other huge pieces of construction equipment were our playground. "Let's play horses," I shouted to Gaby one day. Playing horses meant galloping around and whinnying. Gaby was flabbergasted and not a little disdainful. Pretending was not her long suit. She still remembers that exchange and recalled it on a recent visit. My husband and I had suggested that we all go out to see a movie, and our choice was *The Green Knight*, an epic medieval fantasy adapted from "Sir Gawain and the Green Knight." Gaby was adamant. No, absolutely not. And she explained herself: "I don't like whimsy." It was such an odd phrasing, and we pressed her on what she meant by whimsy. She said she only liked movies—and, by implication, novels—about what she called "real things." Until she retired, Gaby held a highly responsible position at a private girl's school in Montreal, where she specialized in creating programs for girls with learning challenges. Because she has an analytical view of the mind—she can be quick to label small quirks as OCD or ADHD—it was a line of work at which she excelled.

Given this, how did we play together when we were children? How did we reconcile our differences? We roamed the neighbourhood, which was full of other kids our age. We played games with balls and skipping ropes. We rode our bikes. We played board games and went skating. We slept over at each other's houses and made pancakes in the morning. We played with our Barbie dolls, but, given Gaby's aversion to make-believe, only by changing their clothes, not by inventing lives and social interactions for them.

I'm still puzzling over Gaby's use of the word *whimsy*. It is, in a way, a very whimsical way of expressing her dislike of fantasy and other forms of highly imaginative creative work. Much to my surprise, the *Oxford English Dictionary* regards *whimsy* as a mostly archaic and obsolete word. The first definition offered by the dictionary is "Dizziness, giddiness, vertigo. *Obsolete*." You have to move down to definition 3b to find a quote that approximates Gaby's understanding of the word. The quote is from J. Glanvill's 1680 *Saducismus Triumphatus*, "All this is Whimsey and Fiction."

I wonder, would Gaby regard the movie *Harvey* as an example of whimsy? Is *Harvey* whimsical? On the surface, yes, absolutely. The plot moves at a giddy pace, from one farcical situation to another. But beneath all the madcap action, the movie has a critical edge. In the guise of comedy, it paints a horrific picture of the emerging power of the psychiatrist in postwar American culture.

When Dr. Sutherland, the resident psychiatrist of Chumley's Rest Home, cries out "Sound the gong. We mustn't let that woman leave the grounds," Veta is literally hoisted up and carried away by the sanitorium's orderly. She is locked into a soundproof room and stripped. When she is finally released, she staggers home, claiming that a "white slaver" had grabbed her. "He took me upstairs," she says, "and he took off all my clothes, then he dunked me down in a tub of water." This is just one of the institutional practices that sociologist Erving Goffman would, only a handful of years later, say was designed to "mortify" the inmate. Additionally, Veta points out that Dr. Sutherland had simply let Elwood go. "They're not interested in men in places like that," she says. Both Dr. Sutherland and Dr. Chumley, blinded by their training, repeatedly drown out the voices of Veta, Nurse Kelly, and even Mrs. Chumley, and remain blithely oblivious to what is staring them in the face.

What Elwood P. Dowd offers is an alternative masculinity, attentive and unfailingly polite, interested in the backstories of everyone he encounters. He is the still centre of the hectic world of the film. In spite of the endless rounds of martinis, he exhibits greater self-knowledge than either of the psychiatrists. "I've wrestled with reality for thirty-five years, Doctor, and I'm happy to say I've definitely won out over it." *Harvey* signals its motif in a small scene, easily missed. While Veta telephones the sanitorium to arrange to have Elwood committed, he retreats to the library, pulls out his hip flask, and takes a book from the shelves. It is Jane Austen's *Sense and Sensibility*. Elwood is firmly on the side of sensibility.

I wonder if Gaby's antipathy to "whimsy," the way in which she plants her feet so firmly in the realm of "sense," masks an imagination that frightens her. When we were ten or eleven, there was a terrible house fire across the street from our school. A child and a pregnant woman died. Gaby was traumatized by it, and haunted by the spectre of mortality it presented. She couldn't stop imagining what it would be like to be dead. At night, her teeth literally chattered with fear until her older brother discovered this and gave her a pencil to bite down on. For most of her adult years she was afraid to fly. This lasted until about fifteen years ago, when her husband, her high school sweetheart, died of a sudden and aggressive glioblastoma, and she began spending big chunks of her school breaks, summer and winter, flying, not only across the country, but to Europe and the Caribbean. Her Notre-Dame-de-Grâce house felt too empty. It took the lockdowns of COVID to fully reconcile her to her garden, her house, her neighbourhood, and she managed the pandemic with good grace and, dare I say it, imagination. Underneath the disavowal of whimsy, the insistence on "real things," lies a beating and vulnerable sensibility. For all my galloping and whinnying and my invisible Scottish terrier, I was not the one lying awake at night, teeth chattering, imagining myself dead. That would come later.

# Me and Not-Me

*I began this story one week ago, not knowing whether I would go through with it.*

Annie Ernaux, Happening

ON JUNE 24, 2022, THE US SUPREME COURT OVER-
turned its own 1973 decision in *Roe v. Wade*, the decision that
protected a woman's right to have an abortion. The court's
1973 finding was grounded in the Fourteenth Amendment
to the American Constitution, the amendment that famously guarantees that "No State shall make or enforce any law
which shall abridge the privileges or immunities of citizens
of the United States; nor shall any State deprive any person
of life, liberty, or property, without due process of law; nor
deny to any person within its jurisdiction the equal protection
of the laws." *Roe v. Wade* argued that due process included
the right to privacy, which in turn protected a woman's right
to an abortion. The 2022 decision found no such constitu-
tional right; nor was there anything "in the Nation's history
and tradition" that could be understood to presume such a
right. The Supreme Court therefore returned "the authority
to regulate abortion... to the people and their elected repre-
sentatives," that is, to the state legislatures. And now, in many
states, that same Fourteenth Amendment is being wielded as
an instrument to restrict the rights of women.

In the wake of the 2022 decision, Kate Zernike of the *New York Times* published an article titled "Is a Fetus a Person?" The article explores the ways in which anti-abortion activists in the United States are pressing state legislatures to pass so-called fetal personhood laws, "laws that grant fetuses the same legal rights and protections as any person." In the state of Georgia, for example, fetuses are "eligible for child support payments and tax exemptions"; they are to be "counted in 'population-based determinations'" that could influence voting maps or the distribution of state money. It is obvious that fetal personhood laws impinge upon a woman's right to bodily self-determination. They also have the potential to criminalize women for using drugs, or neglecting prenatal care, or for making health decisions that put their own well-being, and sometimes their very lives, above that of the fetus.

The 2019 Georgia law, the Living Infants Fairness and Equality (LIFE) Act, aims to protect the "unborn child" which it defines as "a member of the species Homo sapiens at any stage of development who is carried in the womb." In spite of the law's deliberate use of words, like *infant* and *child* and *womb*, that normally carry enormous emotional weight, it's an awkward and curiously unfeeling definition. Its reference to "the species Homo sapiens" is weirdly taxonomic, intended perhaps to lend a veneer of scientific precision to the messy and contested question of personhood. If a fetus is a person, what kind of person is it? According to the Georgia law, it is first and foremost a citizen: a political, economic, and enumerative person. This is obviously not how any woman carrying a fetus experiences it or imagines it.

I read the *New York Times* article around the same time that I read *Happening* by Annie Ernaux (winner of the 2022

Nobel Prize for Literature), a harrowing account of her, then illegal, 1963 abortion. Ernaux's experience of the fetus is unequivocal: "To convey my predicament, I never resorted to descriptive terms or expressions such as 'I'm expecting,' 'pregnant' or 'pregnancy.' They endorsed a future that would never materialize. There was no point in naming something that I was planning to get rid of. In my diary I would write, 'it' or 'that thing,' only once 'pregnant.'" The fetus is alien, inanimate, a thing. For Ernaux it was the illegality of abortion in France at that time that was the salient issue, her experience defined by its "clandestinity." Writing about it—in spite of the fact that "this narrative is dragging me along in a direction I have not chosen"—is for her a moral act, a way of ensuring that the history of women's suffering is not erased with the passage of time and new laws. She refuses to "be guilty of silencing the lives of women."

Ernaux was twenty-three when she had an abortion. I was not quite eighteen. She kept a diary and an appointment book which she was able to draw on when she wrote *Happening.* "True memory," she says, "has to be material." I kept no record and I find that my own memory is profoundly fragmentary. I have to reconstruct even the year in which it happened; the month is completely lost to me. When I finally sat down to write *this*, I was convinced that I had made notes over the last several months, ideas about how to approach this episode in my life, key phrases that would unlock the strongbox of lost things. I searched every corner of my computer, but there was nothing.

Here is what I do know. I became pregnant the first time I had fully penetrative sex. It happened when I was visiting my boyfriend who had taken a job in Labrador. I flew out to visit him, an act of unimaginable defiance against my parents.

My first boyfriend, my first plane ride, my first experience of sex, even my first coffee which I drank on the plane, black, a revelation. The coffee is vivid, a visceral memory, and yet I struggle to remember the broader shape of my life then.

I had dropped out of school some time earlier and held a series of low-paying jobs. I manage to wrest the memory of the job I held—when? in the spring?—only by remembering the pay phones I used to arrange the abortion. They were outside the women's toilets in the shopping mall near my workplace. There was no way I could make those phone calls from home, from my parents' home. The pay phones were also where I told my boyfriend that I was pregnant. "Do you want me to marry you?" he asked. I believed I was passionately in love with him but I was shocked that he could even imagine that we might marry. I might have fallen out of love with him in that moment. But I can't remember when we broke up or how. Did I break up with him? Did he break up with me? Did the relationship simply dwindle away, victim of distance and something like shock or distress?

But I'm jumping ahead. Shortly after I got back from Labrador I began to feel unwell. I think it never really occurred to me that I could be pregnant, an ignorance or refusal that emerges in so many young women's abortion narratives. I made an appointment with our family doctor who, as it happened, was on leave at the time. A young locum was filling in for him. He sat me down and told me I was pregnant. I wish I could remember my reaction. Did the world collapse beneath my feet? I don't know. He asked if I wanted to have the baby. No, I said. I told him that if my parents knew, I was sure they would send me to a home for unwed mothers and make me give the baby up. It was unthinkable then, in 1970, that a girl might keep her child. And I would not bear a child for someone else. I told him that I wanted to go back to school, to live on a kibbutz. I never did live on a kibbutz but I did go back to school... a lot, eventually earning my PhD. The young locum gave me the telephone number of a McGill University women's group.

This part of the story, with the help of the internet, I can reconstruct accurately. The group was the Montreal Women's Liberation Movement and they operated out of the Women's Centre, located in a historic greystone building on Ste Famille St. There they managed abortion referral services for the clinic that Henry Morgentaler had opened in the east end of Montreal only a year earlier. That was the same year that the Canadian Parliament passed amendments to the Criminal Code that decriminalized homosexuality, permitted abortions under certain highly restricted conditions, and decriminalized the sale of contraceptives. Was I aware of any of this? I don't know.

I telephoned the Women's Centre from the pay phones. They asked how far along was the pregnancy and arranged for payment adjusted to my income. And then my boyfriend and I were there, with another couple who struck me as quite a bit older though they were probably in their twenties. The very serious young women at the centre—I imagine they may have been the same age as the undergraduates I would go on to teach—described to us the procedure, vacuum curettage, and showed us diagrams. They gave us the address of the clinic and advice about bus routes. We travelled with the other couple. Why was my boyfriend there? Had he travelled from Labrador to be with me or was this an already planned and coincidental holiday? I don't remember. I do remember that the bus took us past a cemetery and my boyfriend commented on the aptness of that. In that moment, I hated him.

It was not the last time I would feel something like a cold conviction, or even a cold fury, a kind of steel rod somewhere in the vicinity of my solar plexus. You get to go this far, I would think, but no further.

Now we are in the clinic, an ordinary doctor's clinic occupying a small house on an ordinary street. Suddenly there is a commotion. A young boy has been hit by a car and police officers bring him into the clinic. The woman we travelled with is visibly upset and frightened. I don't recall feeling anything. Dr. Morgentaler emerges and sees to the boy. It occurs to me many years later that of course the police knew what went on in that clinic. Only a few weeks later, they are required to raid it and press charges. Juries refuse to convict.

I remember little of the procedure. I don't recall any significant discomfort. Dr. Morgentaler was kind, as was the grey-haired nurse who patted my hand and told me I was brave.

But what of the fetus? Here's the thing. I felt all along that the fetus and I were in it together, we were a unit. I liked the fetus. I thought about it. I lay in bed at night and put my hands on my stomach. The fetus, at that stage of things, was both me and not-me but mostly me. As mostly me, it wished me well and wanted what was best for me. This may seem delusional, wishful thinking, magical thinking. But my feeling about it has never changed. I continue to feel tenderly toward the fetus. If the pregnancy had happened even a handful of years later, if I could have had and kept the child, things might have been different. But they weren't.

While I obviously don't share the assumptions of the anti-abortionists behind the fetal personhood movement, I also don't share Ernaux's sense of the fetus as "that thing." But writing this has made me realize the degree to which, like Ernaux, I have been shaped by what she called the "clandestinity" of abortion and especially of an illegal abortion. It is something one is alone with. Paradoxically, though, that aloneness also created in me what I now think of as a compulsion to confess. For years I felt that any new friend or boyfriend had a right to know what I had done, in case they had qualms or moral reservations. I like to think that I was motivated by pride in who I was and the decisions I made, and not by a desire to be punished. But I don't know.

What I do know is that I owe my life, the life I have made, the person I have been, to a handful of strangers: the young locum who briefly occupied my family doctor's practice; the fierce young women of the Montreal Women's Liberation Movement; and, most of all, Dr. Henry Morgentaler.

While I was writing this, I dreamed that I was attacked by a bear. The attack left me with the skin flayed off my body and yet I managed to struggle to the curb and wait for the ambulance. When the EMS workers arrived, they grilled me: Is the bear still in the building? Where is the bear now? Throughout this ordeal a young woman remained by my side, supporting me. She was a student in my department's graduate program and we have the same first name.

# Poetry

THE INTERNET HAS COUGHED UP A 1977 photograph of me from the Concordia University student newspaper. The photo takes up a good one third of the page, and it shows me accepting a poetry award from the university rector. My hand is extended, as is that of the rector, but it's a bit unclear whether I am reaching for the handshake or for a piece of paper that memory tells me was a cheque for a hundred dollars. There were twenty-two prizes awarded at that year's Festival for Creative Work in the Arts, and my friend Dana and I each bagged one: poetry for me, fiction for her. I am slim and pretty, my hair in a short bob. Even though the photo is dark, I can make out the outfit I am wearing. It is my favourite: a loose, mid-calf length, dark brown jumper which I wear with tall leather boots. It has big patch pockets on the front. I'm wearing it over a turtleneck sweater, the sleeves pushed up to my elbows. Not long from now, this is the outfit I will wear on my first day as a graduate teaching assistant. I loved that outfit, and I would be wearing it right now, if I could.

Dana has a much better memory for clothes than I do. A handful of months ago, she recalled one of our earliest encounters as first year undergraduates. "You with your pixie cut hairdo and brown turtleneck sweater," she wrote. "You're sitting in one of those chair/desk combos tapping your pen lightly against the cover of a Hilroy notebook, waiting for the old fart to come in and start his lecture." Neither of us can remember the name of that old fart, though we do recall his very loud voice, and the shower of spit that we shrank from whenever he spoke. As for Dana's own outfit: "Me in my mid-calf, A-line denim skirt and blue serge vest over candy-striped cotton. My signature look for that era."

When did I begin to think of myself as a poet? Certainly, by the time I was in high school, though I haven't retained any of my poems from that period. I took a creative writing class in CEGEP and the teacher treated me like a poet. She may even have said the magic words, "As a poet, you...." I began to send my work out to little magazines. At some point, I wised up and sent out a handful of poems under the name J. Wallace. One was accepted and published in the *Canadian Forum*, a highly regarded political, literary, and cultural monthly magazine and a great address for a young poet. But then I felt badly about disguising my gender and I reverted to what I have always considered to be my unfortunately hyphenated, and thereby undignified, first name. In university, I volunteered for the student literary magazine and was bemused by some of the young men in our group. I remember one in particular whose ambition was to be a fellow at Massey College at the University of Toronto, and to sit at high table. His was very much an academic-gown-and-tweed-jacket ideal of the literary life, just one of many models available to young men at the time. We may not have had as many literary foremothers, but nevertheless it was a good time in which to be an aspiring woman poet in Canada. Our numbers were fewer, but they were fearless: Margaret Atwood, Susan Musgrave, Gwendolyn MacEwen, Dorothy Livesay.

I came belatedly to Ann Patchett's *Truth & Beauty: A Friendship,* a memoir the novelist published in 2004 of her seventeen-year friendship with Lucy Grealy, a poet. The book had been out a good fifteen years, but I hadn't seen it. They were both undergraduates at Sarah Lawrence College, where they began to establish themselves in their respective fields, Patchett as a fiction writer, Grealy as a poet. Both were accepted to the prestigious Iowa Writers' Workshop, a graduate level creative writing program, where they shared a ramshackle duplex, grew their complex and intensely intimate friendship, and earned MFAs. Their days and nights were defined by long discussions about the nature of art. They shared *everything* about their new, really new, sexual experiences. They drank, every night they kitchen danced, they wrote. They were exuberantly in their early twenties.

Perhaps it is not surprising that *Truth & Beauty* didn't catch my attention at the time of its publication. Looking back, I see that it received fewer and shorter reviews than I would have expected, given Patchett's status as a novelist. She had, after all, already won the PEN/Faulkner Award and the Orange Prize for *Bel Canto.* But there is something deeply unsettling about the book, a powerful love story to Lucy Grealy. Diagnosed as a young girl with Ewing's sarcoma, a rare bone and soft tissue cancer, Grealy underwent years of radiation and chemotherapy. Years and still more years of largely unsuccessful reconstructive facial surgery followed. The damage to her jaw left her almost toothless, unable to eat anything but tablespoons of soft food, unable to kiss or close her mouth properly. She remained as small as a child, and with a child's insatiable hunger. She needed to be the centre of attention and she needed unconditional love, which she found from Patchett. Grealy fastened onto Patchett like a tiny, voracious limpet, jealous of other claims on her friend's attention. In company, Grealy would crawl into Patchett's lap, rest her head on her chest, eat off her plate. In spite of all this—or maybe because of all this, her unquenchable appetite for everything: sex, art, attention, fame—Grealy was charismatic and popular, a kind of minor celebrity everywhere she lived.

I finally came across the book at the public library, turned face outward on one of the shelves in the Our Staff Recommends section. What grabbed my attention was the basic premise of the memoir: the friendship between two young women, one of them a fiction writer, the other a poet.

Dana and me.

In almost every way, we could not have been more different than Patchett and Grealy. As Dana wrote, in some heat, after reading *Truth & Beauty*, "which one of us would have been Grealy!!!!" Dana is a restrained and elegant writer, and so the extravagance of four exclamation marks was a sign of just how much she disliked the book. "What about Grealy," she stormed, "made putting up with all her shit worthwhile?" Indeed, there was a lot of shit. The second half of *Truth & Beauty* traces Grealy's sharp spiral downwards, much of it driven by her hubristic insistence on more and riskier surgeries, surgeries that she anticipated would finally bring her the True Love she fantasized. Instead, they left her in enormous pain and, combined with her habitual profligacy, enormous debt, much of it paid off by Patchett, the self-described ant to Grealy's grasshopper, the tortoise to her hare. Eventually, predictably, Grealy drifts to heroin. Her death, at thirty-nine, was ruled an accidental overdose.

●●●

DANA'S SHOCKED DISAVOWAL OF ANY SIMILARITY
between our friendship and that of Patchett and Grealy made
good sense. The differences were both sociological and mundane. Born a decade later than us, they were shaped by the
proliferation of MFA writing programs in the US, as well as
by a steady source of endowed fellowships and workshops,
not to mention the more expansive American publication environment. Dana and I were the cultural, though not financial,
beneficiaries of a new and exciting Canadian literature scene.
This meant excellent visiting author programs. We attended
readings by "the best of our generation," to paraphrase Allen
Ginsberg, making it easier to imagine ourselves as writers.
Unlike Patchett and Grealy, we had both been out of school
for a while, returning as slightly older students. We were already partnered with the young men who would become our
first husbands; as a result, our friendship did not share the intense exclusivity, in a way the *girlishness*, of theirs. We didn't
try on each other's clothes. We were, in many ways, less naive.

So why was I, so many years later, caught up in their story?

I remember the first time I visited Dana and her boyfriend
in their small apartment in the Queen Mary neighbourhood.
Their fridge was papered, top to bottom, in *New Yorker* magazine covers. Dana made shepherd's pie for dinner, tucking
peas under the mashed potato covering instead of what I
considered the more canonical creamed corn. I came away
from the evening with two strong impressions. The first was
the confidence suggested by the *New Yorker* magazine covers.
This was the world Dana *intended* to inhabit. The second is
more quixotic: that there's something about Dana, whether
in that tiny apartment or her now spacious Toronto home,

that has the feel of playing house. Is it the pleasure she takes in her things, her pots and pans and, later, her babies? Her pride in her tasteful interiors and her gardens? Her sense of herself as a wife?

I was not living with my boyfriend but in a small studio apartment a couple of blocks from Concordia's west end Loyola Campus. I had a single bed, my parents' old Arborite kitchen table, two kitchen chairs, a rocking chair, and my childhood bureau. A radio. That was it. But it was mine, hard won by hours in the typing pool. That was another thing that Dana and I had in common. We were both self-supporting through our undergraduate degrees. While I typed, she cleaned in a geriatric home or worked as a gas station attendant or served as a receptionist to a lecherous eyeglasses salesman.

There were obvious differences between us. Dana was the child of Holocaust survivors. Having escaped the concentration camps, remarried, and started a new family, her parents were then forced to flee the Hungarian Revolution, first to London and then to Montreal. Dana arrived in Montreal as a child of five. I was the child of newly middle-class Anglo Montrealers, who were struggling to assimilate to nothing more arduous than a West Island suburb. Dana's teenage rebellion was more pronounced and adventurous than mine. Fully adopting the hippy ethos that I only aspired to—my nose pressed against the phantasmagoric hippy plate glass window—she left school and hitchhiked coast to coast. When she was ready to settle down again, she attended the New School at Dawson College CEGEP, a school dedicated to humanistic learning, small classes, connecting the personal to the political. There she was taken under the wing of Greta Nemiroff, one of the most charismatic feminist teachers in Montreal.

Our paths began to split when we completed our undergraduate degrees, both of us leaving Montreal, never to live there again. Following her craft, Dana attended the creative writing program at the University of Windsor, working under the prominent novelist Joyce Carol Oates. I opted for the academic route, beginning my MA and going on to the PhD at York University in Toronto. This was the beginning of what evolved into a largely epistolary friendship, punctuated by visits back and forth between our various cities. Two scenes stand out for me. It is Dana who planted the first in my mind. She recalls us sitting in an empty Loyola classroom, waiting for the other students, waiting for the professor. I stepped up to the chalkboard, turned toward the classroom, and began a faux lecture. She knew then, she said, that I was destined to be an academic.

The other scene is the truly horrible little apartment that Dana and her boyfriend were able to secure in Windsor. It was one half of a tiny bungalow: a kitchen, a bedroom, a living room… and a shared bathroom. Shared with a not entirely clean young man. I took the clattery old train down from Toronto to help Dana clean and scrub their "bohemian" abode, and then sat late at night in the kitchen while she cut pieces of cheese into tiny little squares, centred them on bits of Chex cereal, and popped the whole thing in the oven. Our cleaning, combined with Dana's commitment to lovely interiors, must have done the trick, because her first letter from Windsor reported that the boyfriend "liked the house very much." They discovered jazz, the art gallery, the nearby river. They made a life for themselves.

●●●

BUT WHAT OF POETRY? THE FIRST POEMS I FELL IN love with, in order, were Edward Lear's "The Owl and the Pussy Cat" and Bliss Carman's "Low Tide on Grand Pré." The first is clearly a work of genius and I make no apology. As for "Low Tide on Grand Pré," yes, there's the insistent iambic tetrameter and the rigid rhyme scheme and the repetition of the same word at the end of every second and fifth line. Blah blah blah. But there's also some kind of big whoosh running underneath it all that is unaccounted for by technique alone, and the whoosh is what I was after, it was what I waited for. Once I found the right whoosh for what I needed to say, I was in the groove. It was not always a comfortable groove—as with so many young poets, my subject matter was personal— but I counted on it.

Whooshing and intellectual work make uncomfortable bedfellows, at least in my head. Over the years, poetry, like Puff the magic dragon, slowly slipped away. I still wrote and published the occasional poem, but I was no longer a poet. I can't say I wasn't warned. Early in my first semester of graduate school, I wrote to Dana to say that maybe I wasn't cut out for academic life after all. I was dismayed by what I described as the "glass bead game" quality of what I still quaintly referred to as "literary criticism." One of my professors, Ernest Griffin—English, slightly tubby, tweed jacket, tie, woollen vest—gently suggested to me that the university was, after all, a place of abstract thought. In time, I found my way into the literary theoretical glass bead game and, later, to a research program that, for me, forged that crucial link between lived lives and the writing they produced.

I thought I could have both, the poetry and the scholarly work. I certainly wanted both and anticipated that university life would support them. But it turns out that poetry, for me, was a thing of the blood. It couldn't simply be conjured; it had to tap into some kind of rhythmic insistence. Something about academic work, for me, blocked that force.

●–●–●

AND WHAT OF DANA? AFTER WINDSOR, THERE were a couple of years in London, Ontario, while her boyfriend earned his education degree. These were followed, unbelievably, by three years in Grande Prairie, Alberta, where he had secured a teaching position. Smack in the middle of an oil boom, it was a confident and swaggering town of new houses and new trucks. City-girl Dana managed the change with surprising good grace, balking at eating moose meat chili but exulting in the landscape. She reluctantly undertook a miscellaneous series of jobs—everything from advertising paste-up in the backroom of the local newspaper to program advising at the college—always keeping her eye on the ball, the prize, of not working at all but devoting herself to her writing. "Reading," she wrote to me when she was twenty-four, "is my narcotic. And I wish for nothing more than a couch & a book & occasionally a dip of the pen." This was a goal she finally accomplished a few years, a different city, and two children later. It paid off in a major literary award, and a collection of short stories with a very good trade publisher.

But. Isn't there always a "but" for the princess in the tower? The poisoned spindle. The red shoes. The nettles that must be woven into so many clean white shirts. In Dana's case it was her husband. His mental health had long been precarious. It always felt like an accomplishment to make him smile and to hear his wide-mouthed barking laugh. Loose-limbed, he seemed a little surprised by the sound himself. But nothing—not his beloved boys, not his work, not his marriage—could halt the inexorable slide. Dana steered her young family through some terrible years before he succumbed to suicide when the children were still teenagers.

And I didn't know.

How could that be? After eighteen years of letters flying back and forth across the country, over eighty thousand words of support and love and gossip and commentary on one another's dreams and stories and poems. All of it punctuated by highly anticipated in-person visits when we could manage them. How could I not know that Dana's husband had killed himself? I remember the moment I heard about it. The Nova Scotia author Alistair MacLeod was being awarded an honorary doctorate from the University of Alberta and my husband and I were driving him to a reception at the university president's house. Knowing he had taught at the University of Windsor, I asked him if he knew my friend Dana and her husband. "You know he killed himself?" was the reply.

I didn't know.

◉ ◉ ◉

THERE'S A VERY MOVING PASSAGE NEAR THE END of *Truth & Beauty*, its grief and guilt all the more poignant because they are so carefully underplayed. Patchett recalls what talking and being with Grealy had always meant to her: "Whenever I saw her, I felt like I had been living in another country, doing moderately well in another language, and then she showed up speaking English and suddenly I could speak with all the complexity and nuance that I hadn't even realized was gone." Grealy's love affair with heroin meant they could now go weeks without speaking. Indeed, the night that Grealy died, Patchett had been visiting New York for an awards ceremony and, uncharacteristically, hadn't tried to contact her. Who could blame her?

The several-weeks-long lacuna in Patchett and Grealy's relationship was almost twenty years for Dana and me. Here is my side of it. I have never heard Dana's.

Our lives, predictably, grew apart. Dana, as I understood it, stayed home and managed her family, driving her boys across the city to their progressive school, squiring them to their sporting activities, hosting parties and sleepovers, and hanging out with other "Moms." I was beginning to build my career, getting research grants, travelling to conferences and archives, taking on increasing administrative responsibilities, juggling a big load of doctoral supervisions. In the middle of all this, the happiness of a new relationship with a good man and a nice kid. In one of my last letters, I wrote this to Dana: "These days my bed seems like Grand Central Station—not nearly as exciting as it sounds. Allie now does 'sleepovers' two or three nights a week (virtually whenever she is with Stephen), and she likes to spend a few minutes in our bed after getting up in the morning (chatting, telling us her dreams, doing calisthenics...). So I spend many mornings squashed into a corner of my bed—upon which sprawl two cats, one kid, and another grownup."

A year later, Stephen and Allie and I travelled to Ontario, a chance for our families and friends to meet. We had a date set up with Dana and her family and then, at the last minute, leaving a message on my parents' answering machine, she cancelled—an unexpected or forgotten sports event involving her boys—but she could set aside some time later for the two of us. I was heartbroken. I thought of all the years I had visited her or picked her up at her apartment or house, and witnessed the latest exploits of the boys, admired their drawings, listened to their songs, saw them in their fresh-from-the-bath pyjamas. And she couldn't make time to meet my new little family?

What I know now is that there are some things you can't write in letters or discuss in a long-distance phone call. The breakdowns. The scenes. The terrible drives to Emergency or worse. I don't blame myself. I don't feel guilty. But my picture was incomplete.

᠅

TURNING FIFTY FELT MOMENTOUS TO ME. TIME'S wingèd chariot, this too too solid flesh, it is the blight man was born for, etc., etc. It seemed to me that I could drop dead at any moment. I thought I had better put at least one or two of my affairs in order, and so I bought a paper shredder and hauled some boxes up from the basement. Stephen was away for a nice chunk of time—mountaineering camp, maybe?—and so down I went, down the wonderland rabbit hole of time, determined to destroy anything that might cause him pain in the event of my sudden demise. There were old photo albums; in particular, there were photos from my first wedding. I examined them all carefully and then... bzzz bzzz bzzz... through the paper shredder. There was one of me that I thought particularly nice and wanted to preserve, and so I carefully cut my brand new, now ex-husband out of it. It seemed like the kind of thing people did only in the movies. There were letters, one a particularly excoriating screed from a former lover, pointing out all my failings and weaknesses. He had small, precise handwriting and I imagined him writing drafts of the thing before sending along the fair copy. I felt enormously indignant when I first got the letter. On rereading it, though, I had to concede that he made several good points. Bzzz bzzz bzzz. If Stephen didn't arrive at any of these unfortunate conclusions for himself, there was no need to add a helping hand. There were letters from my ex-husband, sent during the first summer of our courtship when he was away winterizing his parents' summer cottage. How clear it was, in retrospect, that we were both ambitious, but for very different things. Bzzz bzzz bzzz. Of course, there were old poems and contact sheets from when I kind of took photography in CEGEP; which is to say, from when I snuck into the darkroom. There were letters from Carole, written during what felt like her period of exile in Toronto. And there were letters from Dana. So many letters. As I reread them all, it struck me that I was reading not only personal history, but the social history of a generation of young women. So I typed them all up. I'm a fast typist, but it took up a lot of my spare time that summer.

And then I went looking for her.

I sent a short, rather formal letter to the last address I had for her, a small bungalow in west Toronto. I explained that I had found and typed up her letters to me. Would she like the originals? My letter was returned to sender. Moved. Next, I wrote to her publisher. I explained that I knew they couldn't let me have Dana's address, but maybe they'd be willing to forward a letter? It turned out even her publisher didn't have her new address. That letter, too, was eventually returned. But Dana, at that time, was again writing strongly and productively, and she set up a web-based author's page that allowed people to send her a comment. Finally, I was able to make contact. We emailed back and forth, hesitantly, formally, relaying bits of basic information. Dana typed up my old letters and interleaved them with hers. I flew to Toronto. And then it was as if the twenty years evaporated.

Ours is still a largely epistolary friendship, but without the postage stamps and delayed delivery. We treat email like paper: Dear Dana, Dear Jo-Ann. There are still things that can't be put in writing, and we look forward eagerly to the occasional face-to-face visits.

●  ●  ●

PROFESSOR ERNEST GRIFFIN ONCE SAID TO ME that lyric poetry was a young man's game. Of course, I forgave him the gendered expression. I didn't even point it out. But over the years I have thought many times about what he said. Is it true? Is lyric poetry a young person's genre? W. B. Yeats would disagree. Seamus Heaney would disagree. I think I disagree too.

# LATE

# Melmac

I THINK OF THEM AS THE MELMAC YEARS. THAT makes it sound like a lifetime—my lifetime—ago. In fact, it was only about twenty years ago and the whole thing began innocently enough with the purchase of an already ancient Class C motorhome. It might be kinder to describe the motorhome as "retro," its upholstery, window curtains, and decorative exterior stripes all in the orange and brown so characteristic of its early 1970s vintage. Typical of its class and age, our GMC Aristocrat had a small gas-powered stovetop and oven, a small refrigerator, a small furnace, and a small bathroom with a shower hose. To take a shower, you locked yourself into the telephone booth-sized room, ran the shower curtain across the door, plugged the rubber shower hose into the water tap in the sink, and sat on the closed toilet lid. The water ran down through a drain in the floor into the grey water receptacle under the motorhome. We also had a small microwave oven which, like the shower, was very rarely used.

We almost never stayed at sites with electric plug-ins, much less water hookups. And we didn't travel far, despite our initial fantasies of long road trips down the West Coast. Our old motorhome struggled up even the mildest of hills and so, after a couple of nail-biting trips to the mountains, we restricted ourselves to exploring campgrounds within a three-hour radius of Edmonton. We did our best to turn the motorhome's limitations into an only semi-ironic virtue, practicing what we called "the way of the motorhome." This involved a leisurely pace and a blind eye to the lineup of cars inevitably building up behind us. It was a kind of highway Zen interrupted only by the sound of one of our dogs vomiting behind us. Our dear old Jessie loved road trips, but her stomach didn't.

Our routine never varied. We would pull into a campsite making sure that our biggest window faced the best view. Next, we would level the motorhome. This was a complicated exercise that involved placing a can of Coke on the floor and then inching the Aristocrat backwards and forwards, sticking blocks of wood—essentially large shims—under one tire or another, until the can stopped rolling. Finally, we unpacked. Out came the metal candlesticks and the wax candles. Out came the bottle of wine. Wherever we were, we were probably the classiest act in the whole campground, though, to be honest, we were often the *only* act in the campground, since we much preferred off-season camping. Some of our best times involved wandering across a frozen lake with our dogs, peering into the holes that had been hand augured out by ice fishermen, coming back to the motorhome and cranking up the heat on its little furnace.

What our GMC lacked in oomph it made up for with a pretty good sound system, albeit one that was limited to playing cassettes. So, after walking the dogs, we'd slip in a tape, pour a glass of wine, light the candles (it gets dark early in the off season), and set about making dinner. Dinner which we served on Melmac plates.

Motorhomes are rollicking affairs and china and glass-ware don't survive the road. In the beginning, we invested in a new set of inexpensive Canadian Tire melamine dishes in watermelon colours. They were fine, they were serviceable, but they were... unromantic. Then one day, wandering in a thrift shop, I saw a couple of old Melmac mugs, a couple of cereal bowls, a plate or two. Ooh, I thought, that's more like it. And so it began. My Melmac obsession. My Melmac addiction. I began to haunt the thrift shops, but finding decent Melmac at Goodwill or Value Village or the Bissell Centre was pretty hit-and-miss. Luckily, or unluckily, those were the relatively early days of eBay. That online auctioneer—my accomplice, my enabler, my supplier.

I soon built up a serviceable collection of motorhome Melmac. Some of the items were familiar from my childhood. The sturdy Canadian-made GPL mugs with the art deco–like edges that made them easily stackable. The matching salmon pink or mint green or pale blue cereal bowls and plates, satisfyingly heavy in the hand. The insulated raffia ware drinking glasses—lined with burlap beneath a clear plastic surface, the rims turned gently outward in sunshine colours of coral, yellow and aqua—designed for chilled colas and lemonades on the patios of new suburban developments. Little Melmac juice glasses, standing up straight like child soldiers in the motorhome cupboard. Then it became necessary to have serving bowls, a variety of serving bowls, some of them covered, some shaped like a fat number eight with a dividing line down the middle—carrots on one side, peas on the other. And why not a water jug? Two water jugs? Creamers and sugar bowls? Salt and pepper shakers? Butter dishes? A salad bowl set with built in handles in speckled confetti green? Ice-cream sundae cups? A tiered cake plate? Why not?

The packages arrived from all over the continent and my Melmac collection grew quickly, very quickly. Soon it outgrew the motorhome.

In time my taste became more discerning and, without abandoning the GPL and raffia ware of my childhood, I began to concentrate my efforts on Melmac designed by Russel Wright, a well-respected American mid-century industrial designer who focused on domestic environments. With his wife, Mary, Wright published the influential *Guide to Easier Living* in 1950. The book's main argument was that—in a modern, post-war, post-servant world—"formality is not necessary for beauty."

Russel Wright was the William Morris of plastic and spun aluminum, leading the newly and increasingly well-off middle classes to a modern life that was family focused, casual, easy-care, unbreakable. While he is now perhaps best known for his line of American Modern ceramic dinnerware, it was his Residential line of Melmac dishes that won the Museum of Modern Art's Good Design Award in 1953.

Wright's Melmac dishes are unadorned, fluid and organic; the bowls and creamers extend on one side to small, open, almost wavelike handles, while his oval dinner plates are framed by shallow indented tabs. They feel wonderful in the hand. Produced mostly in the lightly mottled colours of lemon ice, turquoise, salmon red, and sea mist grey, the line takes full advantage of one of Melmac's primary qualities: its mouldability.

Melmac was, in fact, the branded name of the melamine resin produced by American Cyanamid. The company was founded in 1907 as a maker of fertilizer, eventually becoming one of the most diversified chemical manufacturers in the world, with a particular emphasis on pharmaceuticals.

When various moulders, who actually made the sundry plastic products that later filled our motorhome, purchased their powdered melamine resin from American Cyanamid, they were permitted to use the trade name Melmac (the one that manufactured Wright's line was the Northern Industrial Chemical Company). These outfits could also participate in widespread Melmac advertising campaigns that featured in department store displays and in magazines like *Life*. "A new high in beauty... a new low in breakage." "For Christmas Day and Every Day: Boontonware break-resistant Melmac!" "You can be good and carefree... when it's dinnerware molded of Melmac."

When reading these taglines today, it's difficult not to think of Dupont's famously hopeful slogan, "Better things for better living through chemistry." Such optimism dominated the 1950s and 1960s in North America. Is this what attracted me to Melmac? A nostalgia for the postwar promise of easy living, casual elegance, carefree homes? The promise of un-breakability?

The Melmac years were not easy ones for me. I was chairing a large and complex university department with seventy full-time, tenured or tenure-track faculty members, a graduate program with some one hundred and forty students, and an untold number of contract instructors. I had a supportive dean for the first year of my appointment and an antagonistic one for the remainder; he and his associate dean carried an animus toward English studies in general and my department in particular. In spite of that, my colleagues and I accomplished a lot: we concluded a complete overhaul of the undergraduate curriculum and a highly successful external review of the graduate program; we hired over a dozen new colleagues; and we effected a strategic reduction in the teaching load to bring us in line with our peers in the social sciences. It was stressful. Some of my decisions and assessments cost me friendships. And the workload was crushing. At home, I was a half-time stepmother to a child just entering middle school. She was an uncommonly easy child—cheerful, smart, outgoing. But the week-on/week-off zigzaginess of it all—accommodating her vegetarian diet, preparing school lunches, keeping track of laundry and schedules—was... well, zigzaggy. My immune system is normally robust, but I have never been so sick so often as I was during those years. I was not unbreakable.

I guess this might be the time to confess that the Melmac years overlapped with the Occupied Japan years. Not all of the packages arriving from all over the continent contained Melmac. Some contained small figurines, cheaply produced and schmaltzy. Scottie dogs wearing tams and smoking pipes, mallard ducks flying across the wall, cowboys strumming guitars or carrying lassos, tiny planters shaped like carts drawn by mules: these little trinkets were produced between 1945 and 1952, when Japan was under the Allied occupation led by General Douglas MacArthur. As part of the economic recovery plan, munitions factories were repurposed, though the goods they produced for overseas markets had to be stamped with "Made in Occupied Japan" on their base.

I can, with a straight face, justify the Melmac obsession through an appeal to mid-century aesthetics. But the Occupied Japan obsession? What was that all about? On the one hand, both Melmac and Occupied Japan figurines are mass-manufactured goods of the immediate postwar era. On the other hand, they are at opposite ends of the industrial design aesthetic. One is sleek, practical, innovative; the other is derivative, intended only for shallow display. Was I identifying with Japan, constrained to produce sentimental ephemera for distant markets? Writing long reports for external review committees or even detailed annual assessments of seventy colleagues sometimes felt like that. Or was it something about my childhood: those memories of standing on tiptoe in the five-and-dime store, dreaming of buying a little porcelain lady for my mother for Christmas? Or visiting great-aunts and breathing in the smell of doilies and lavender water and admiring the fancy figurines on coffee tables and bureaus?

In his 2008 book, *In the Realm of Hungry Ghosts*, Vancouver physician and addictions expert Gabor Maté describes his collecting classical music CDs as an addiction. It is, of course, a controversial claim but he maintains it seriously. His obsession, he says, meets the criteria: it is compulsive; he has little control over his behaviour, even heading to the music store in the middle of a patient's labour; he relapses in spite of the harm it does to his bank account and his marriage; and he experiences intense craving when he is unable to indulge his passion. By these criteria, mine was not actually an addiction. Nonetheless, by the time the Melmac years came to a natural end, there were a half-dozen big tubs of pieces in the basement, along with a couple of boxes of Occupied Japan figurines. When we sold the house and packed up, I did feel a little pang as we carted evidence of that period off to the neighbourhood charity shop—most of the evidence, anyway. As I type this, I look up to admire the succulent—a little zebra plant—growing in a pot shaped like a black Scottie dog. And, especially when outdoor entertaining season rolls around, I am glad I kept the turquoise Russel Wright dinnerware.

# This Gaiety Would Have Been Mine

IN VIRGINIA WOOLF'S 1925 NOVEL *MRS. DALLOWAY*, the title character, Clarissa, sits in her drawing-room mending the silver-green dress she plans to wear to the party that night. She and her husband Richard, a mid-level member of the Conservative government, are hosting, and Clarissa very much hopes that the prime minister will make an appearance. As she bends to her task, Clarissa loses herself in the moment. "Quiet descended on her, calm, content," writes Woolf, "as her needle, drawing the silk smoothly to its gentle pause, collected the green folds together and attached them, very lightly, to the belt."

Her reverie is interrupted by an unexpected visit from an old beau, someone she has not seen in as many as thirty years. Peter Walsh has returned to England after years abroad to help settle the divorce of a woman he intends to marry. The reunion of Clarissa and Peter is highly charged, emotional, and complicated. Especially because the last time they met—"that awful night," as Peter thinks of it—Clarissa rejected him in favour of the thoroughly decent, though very dull, Richard Dalloway.

Before Richard Dalloway appeared on the scene, Clarissa and Peter enjoyed an almost volatile intimacy. They talked and argued and influenced one another profoundly. "They went in and out of each other's minds without any effort." Yet Clarissa's decision to marry Richard and not Peter makes good sense. She loves society, loves throwing parties, loves a beautiful home and servants, and Richard's position affords her that. And Richard offers her something she values even more, "the privacy of the soul." With Peter "everything had to be shared; everything gone into. And it was intolerable."

Even so, Clarissa has continued over the years, over the decades, to question her decision and justify it to herself. And when Peter suddenly appears in her drawing-room, she feels in her breast "the brandishing of silver-flashing plumes like pampas grass in a tropical gale." She thinks "If I had married him, this gaiety would have been mine all day!"

●●●

MRS. DALLOWAY HAS ACCOMPANIED ME THROUGH-out the greater part of my adult life, keeping step with me for more than forty years. It was the ostensible subject of my now very dated doctoral dissertation, which explored the novel through the lens of what we described then as the "new" French feminist theories of the body. In a way, *Mrs. Dalloway* was an odd choice for this exercise. Woolf's experiments with literary form, her attempt to capture the ways in which "the mind receives a myriad impressions... an incessant shower of innumerable atoms," did rub up well against the *écriture feminine*. On the other hand, Clarissa, though elegant and striking at fifty-two, feels the long-lasting effects of influenza and what may be a related heart condition. She increasingly thinks about death and experiences herself as almost disembodied. "Often now," writes Woolf, "this body she wore... this body, with all its capacities, seemed nothing—nothing at all." While she takes an almost sensual pleasure in everyday activities, like buying flowers, and while she detests organized religion, her priorities could be described as metaphysical and spiritual rather than bodily.

So why did I choose this novel at that time of intensive study, and personal and career formation? I wanted to work on Woolf. I wanted to work on French feminist theory. So I crammed the two things together. And that's as much as I want to think about it now. The thought of cracking open the dusty, bound copy of my dissertation to confirm any of this makes me cringe.

But what a happy choice *Mrs. Dalloway* turned out to be. Over the years, I have taught it, reread it, researched it deeply, and repeatedly turned to it to find expression for something I am going through.

Shortly after taking up my tenure-track position in the Department of English, a young feminist art historian and I undertook a collaborative research project on early twentieth-century women artists and writers. This work took me into archives of all kinds, and it rejigged my research priorities. As a result, the whole universe of the novel was waiting for me when I eventually returned to *Mrs. Dalloway*. Much like invisible ink rising to the surface, Woolf's complex engagement with the social and political issues of her day now revealed itself to me. Clarissa's working-class doppelgänger, the shell-shocked First World War veteran Septimus Smith, is the most obvious expression of the ways in which a historical sensibility undergirds the novel. But contemporary readers would also have known that the unnamed prime minister who does indeed attend Clarissa's party that night in June 1923 would effectively lose the December general election only six months later. Britain would have its first Labour government and the country would arrive at the brink of enormous social change. Loving the research this approach involved, I produced an edition of *Mrs. Dalloway* that—through an introduction, appendices, and footnotes—framed it in its full historical context. I taught the novel numerous times in undergraduate courses on historical methodology.

Most recently, I turned to Woolf to find words to describe what I had just experienced as an invasive and distressing interaction with a health professional. And the words were there. Septimus Smith is about to be committed to a rest cure by his titled Harley Street physician, and soon after he kills himself rather than submit to the doctor's prescription. Like Clarissa, he values "the privacy of the soul." "So he was in their power!" he thinks. "The brute with the red nostrils was snuffling into every secret place!" The words may have been a bit hyperbolic for my situation, perhaps, but they absolutely captured my own resistant state of mind.

But the words from the novel that have resonated with me most over many years are those that appear in Clarissa's mind when she, after their many years apart, again meets Peter. "This gaiety would have been mine all day!" Those words sprang spontaneously into my mind one day in my late thirties, while I was sitting in a lecture hall, listening to a talk by a visiting scholar. I was also watching Stephen, sitting a couple of rows ahead of me, as the sun touched his red hair. We were great friends, going for coffee, gossiping over a drink following department council meetings, dropping in and out of each other's offices, even co-teaching a graduate seminar that explored two previously unrelated areas. In and out of each other's offices and also, like Clarissa and Peter, in and out of each other's minds. We drove together to a friend's cabin in Jasper for a winter weekend, stopping by the highway on the way home to wait out my old car's overheating radiator (yes, in the middle of winter!) and watch the northern lights, an experience that was somehow both ridiculous and profound. We flew together to a conference and played all the stupid games in the Air Canada magazine. No one was more fun than Stephen. We could not have been closer. Except we could.

Stephen wanted a full relationship. I did not. This would not have been my first go-round following the breakup of my marriage, and the thought of Stephen not being in my life, centrally in my life, was heartbreaking. So why was I holding back? Why was I so grudging, even grumpy, about the whole thing? There were, of course, the conventional reasons for caution. I was divorced while he was only newly separated. He had a not-quite ex-wife and a very young daughter, and he was inching toward an arrangement of completely shared custody. But the problem couldn't be located in a sensible assessment of the situation. It took me a long time to figure out that it was probably the sheer certainty of his love for me, his wild enthusiasm for the relationship that put me off. How could I live up to that? How was it possible that it wouldn't smother me, wear me down, wipe me away? This, of course, is what Clarissa fears from a relationship with Peter Walsh, that she will lose the privacy of the soul, though she later wonders whether, in making the sensible decision, she has lost something else. But that day in the lecture hall, unlike Clarissa, and in words very unlike any that she would use, I came to a different conclusion. "Oh, fuck it," I thought. "Let's just do it."

The way has not always been smooth. But it was not smoothness I was after. There are two types of people, a colleague once told me. They come from Genesis. "And Jacob said to Rebekah his mother, Behold, Esau my brother is a hairy man, and I am a smooth man." I did not want a smooth man, and I did not want a smooth relationship. I was after a spark, the kind of spark that is as likely to lead to inane squabbling as anything else. The kind of spark that leads to helpless laughter, as happened at our wedding. We were married in the living room of our small bungalow, our little dog yapping excitedly in the background, and we couldn't get the words spoken by the inept priest played by Rowan Atkinson in *Four Weddings and a Funeral* out of our minds: "I do take thee... to be my awful wedded wife."

I sometimes think that in Stephen I have found a worthy adversary. We are both professors of English and we like to "use our words." Arguments can begin in verbal foreplay, a progressive amping up in volume, until a crescendo of one of us yelling "Fuck you!", the other responding "No, fuck *you!*" which breaks the tension and we again stand revealed to one another in all our absurdity. I have often been an "awful wife," carping, critical, grouchy. He is often distracted, pretending to listen to me when he clearly isn't. We talk to each other all day long. We even text from room to room.

This is gaiety, of a fashion. And it is mine.

# Virginia Woolf's Commas

SEVERAL YEARS AGO, I PREPARED A SCHOLARLY edition of Virginia Woolf's 1925 novel *Mrs. Dalloway* for Broadview Press, intended for use in the classroom but also for interested "common readers." Among my tasks was choosing an edition of the novel and digitizing it. The two obvious contenders were the first edition produced by Woolf's own Hogarth Press and that of her American publisher Harcourt Brace. There are some minor, though not insignificant, differences between the two editions but, to be honest, my choice of the Hogarth edition was largely sentimental. As E. F. Shields puts it in her exhaustive essay on "The American Edition of *Mrs. Dalloway*," both "can legitimately claim to be authoritative first editions."

When it came to digitizing the novel, the normal practice would have been to use OCR (optical character recognition) software: scanning the book page by page and then running the software to convert it into a Word document. This has the advantage of speed, but it has an accuracy rating of between eighty-one and ninety-nine percent depending on the source material. In other words, what you gain in speed you have to make up in painstaking proofreading and correction. I chose to enter the text the old-fashioned way, by typing it in myself.

I am a fast and pretty accurate typist, perhaps the only characteristic I share with Northrop Frye who, in 1929, travelled to Toronto from his home in New Brunswick to compete in a national speed-typing contest. He came second. I don't know how Frye came to be such an accomplished typist—seventy-two words a minute—but my own typing history is straightforward. When I was in high school in Montreal in the late 1960s, there were few optional courses available if, like me, you had no aptitude for maths or science. In grade ten my choices were Latin or typing. My parents told me to choose typing so that I would always have a way of supporting myself if my husband died. That was their reason and I suppose, given their own backgrounds, it wasn't unreasonable. Typing class meant a room of girls working heavy old manual typewriters, pieces of paper taped to the machines and extending over our hands so that we couldn't see the keyboard. "ASDF JKL;" is still burned into my brain and my fingers.

I sometimes wonder whether Latin would have been more useful to me than typing, but the fact is that I quite like typing. There is something satisfying about the exercise of that kind of fine muscle memory. And typing did support me through my undergraduate degree. When classes were over in the spring, I would head over to Kelly Girl Services and the agency would assign me temp jobs. One of my earliest, for the Sun Life Assurance Company, lasted the whole summer. I was sent to their massive, birthday cake-shaped building on Dominion Square (as it was then called) in downtown Montreal. The typists, and there were many of us, sat in row upon rows in a huge, brightly lit room. We were each assigned a desk and typewriter, but that was as personal as it got. I don't recall a single conversation with my neighbouring typists, though I must have spoken to them. I do recall correcting the grammar and spelling of the letters I typed, though my changes were never acknowledged by the insurance agents. Montreal wasn't T. S. Eliot's "Unreal City," and the insurance agents were not quite carbuncular clerks, but it was a soulless job. The only perk was the free hot lunch that Sun Life provided to all its employees.

A couple of years later my father got me a job as a summer typist at his insurance brokerage in Place du Canada, not far from the Sun Life Building. There, under the supervision of Monsieur Lefebvre, I typed multicopy forms in the personal insurance division. It was tedious work, but occasionally something would catch my attention—the contents of a rich person's home, for instance. I would type up all their paintings, jewellery, and furs. The filing clerks, all women, were kind to me, in part because they liked my father, who by then was a vice president with an office in the executive suite. (They liked him because when he arrived in the morning he filled his own kettle in the staff kitchen and made his own instant coffee, not relying on his secretary to do it.) The job extended into the academic year, and depending on my university schedule, I worked either three half days or two full days a week. One effect of this was to limit my sartorial choices. Clothes had to be suitable for the office and for college, and so I was never able to indulge my passion for peasant skirts and blouses, army surplus jackets, head scarves, and tinkling jewellery. The kinds of things I thought a poet should wear.

Office work taught me that I didn't want a nine-to-five job. I didn't want to be in the crush of commuters riding up the escalator from the train station in the morning and down the escalator in the evening. I didn't want to go up and down elevators at the same time every day. I didn't want to line up at lunchtime to do my banking. I didn't want to wear office clothes. I didn't want to be surrounded by men in suits. I didn't want any part of that world. So when, at the end of my BA and after I had already decided to go on to the MA, my father asked me to consider becoming an insurance agent—in the personal insurance division—I was both taken aback and adamant. No, absolutely not. I may also have been a little touched by the suggestion. I hope I was. He was asking me to follow in his footsteps, after all. But personal insurance was the women's side of the game. My father, like the other men in the executive suite, negotiated insurance for huge corporations. Still, he saw something in me and thought I could be more than a secretary.

What does any of this have to do with Virginia Woolf's commas? Only typing. I typed *Mrs. Dalloway* from beginning to end. There is something surprisingly intimate about entering text in this way. I knew that by typing up the novel I would refamiliarize myself with it. What I didn't anticipate was that I would learn something about the minutiae of Woolf's style, and in particular her often eccentric use of commas, semicolons, and other punctuation marks. Here is one example, chosen at random. Rezia is in Regent's Park with Septimus. She remembers her life in Italy and speaks aloud to herself. "Her words faded. So a rocket fades. Its sparks, having grazed their way into the night, surrender to it, dark descends, pours over the outlines of houses and towers; bleak hill-sides soften and fall in." Why insert a semi-colon after "houses and towers" but not after "surrender to it"? Not infrequently, Woolf uses a semicolon where you might anticipate a comma and she often inserts a comma unexpectedly. The element of anticipation is important here, because typing, which relies on muscle memory, is in many ways about anticipation, it is the expression of anticipation. Even as I type the word *anticipation*, my fingers prepare themselves for the falling into place of that concluding *tion* which, after years of entering such words, falls trippingly from the fingers. As Stephen pointed out to me, "Language is a kind of music and typing is a way of playing it." Entering *Mrs. Dalloway* manually, by typing it, produces a physical response to Woolf's style as the fingers struggle not to enter a comma where a comma would ordinarily appear. For a while I thought it might be interesting to work up a scholarly article on Woolf's often eccentric punctuation, but then I thought better of it. It was not an article I would particularly want to read.

# I Don't Care About This Anymore

I DON'T CARE ABOUT THIS ANYMORE. SHOULD I?
Do I care that I don't care? These thoughts occur to me as I
walk around the book section of the Tate Modern gift shop
in London. I so completely don't care that it's difficult to
remember why I cared in the first place or what that caring
felt like. I think it felt full of passionate intensity. But also,
anxiety, a near desperate worry that I'd never measure up,
I'd never get it right, never *really* figure it out. What began as
lively curiosity became a commitment and a responsibility, a
kind of burden. No, I'm not referring to a love affair gone bad
but to "theory," as we called it then, and maybe we still do.
But I don't care. And my not caring is visceral, a deep physical
aversion. I shy away from those shelves like a dog recoiling
from the smell of a cut lemon. *Žižek on Race. Notes Toward
a Performative Theory of Assembly. Unbecoming Language:
Anti-Identitarian French Feminist Fictions. Entering Trans-
masculinity: The Inevitability of Discourse.*

No, please, no.

I pause briefly at a book called *Reading Lacan's Ecrits.*
This is because I have just finished reading a long article

about Simone de Beauvoir in the *London Review of Books*, in which the author mentions in passing that one of Beauvoir's numerous lovers—shared, like so many, with Sartre—underwent psychoanalysis with Lacan. This piques my interest. The crazy, messy, complicated humanity of it all. Bodies in cafés, bodies in bedrooms, bodies smoking cigarettes at typewriters, bodies in the offices of psychoanalysts. But wait. Did Lacan meet with his patients in an ordinary office? We know what Freud's Viennese consulting room looked like, with its oriental carpets and pillows and stone figures, all those classical heads on their little pedestals. We can guess that it smelled like cigars and perhaps, later in Freud's life, like his dog Jofi who sat in on sessions and got up and stretched to signal that the fifty minutes were over.

I google "Jacques Lacan's consulting room" and I get only images of the great man himself, the dark circles under his eyes, the deep cleft in his chin. I google "what was it like to be psychoanalyzed by Jacques Lacan?" but the internet doesn't seem to know or care, though it does remind me that "the unconscious is structured like a language," and I conclude that being psychoanalyzed by Lacan must have been a pretty bloodless affair. I can't help imagining a startlingly white laboratory and a faint but pervasive smell of formaldehyde. I could look into the question more deeply, but I find that I no longer care.

I *do* care about Simone de Beauvoir. I do care that I bought my first copy of *The Second Sex* in the neighbourhood drug store which sold a wildly unpredictable assortment of books and comics, everything from Batman to Beauvoir. I *do* care that it was the austerely beige Knopf Doubleday paperback edition, boldly subtitled "the classic manifesto of the liberated woman." I don't care that my first reading of *The Second*

*Sex* was in the now discredited translation by zoologist H. M. Parshley. I *don't* care about that because reading *The Second Sex* wasn't about rigorously tracing the philosophical roots of the positions that Beauvoir argued. The book was a slingshot, a springboard, a door opening, a spotlight shining, something clicking firmly into place, never to be dislodged. "One is not born, but rather becomes, a woman." Not theory, but life.

"Not theory, but life." Do I even know what I mean by that? It has a vaguely Woolfian inflection so maybe I'm just being derivative. And I *do* care about Virginia Woolf. I care about *To the Lighthouse*'s Lily Briscoe standing before her unfinished canvas and thinking "What is the meaning of life? That was all—a simple question; one that tended to close in on one with years." What is the meaning of life?—a simple question that Theory, the theory of my intellectual age, does not care to answer.

As *my* years closed in, I stood in the office that had been my academic home for twenty-eight years and decided what to toss out and what to keep. My fat teaching file on Ezra Pound went straight into the recycling bin. There you go, you old fascist; I'll never have to think about you again. Then I turned to the books. All the poetry stayed (except Ezra Pound's). All of Bloomsbury stayed. All the literary biographies (except Ezra Pound's). All of D. H. Lawrence because even though he desperately wanted to have the heart of a fascist, the lunatic enormity of his emotions meant he couldn't quite carry it off. All of Doris Lessing because she was a fearless explorer of worlds—political, psychic, spiritual, even extraterrestrial. And, now residing on the top shelf of one of the bookcases in my home office, a small handful of disparate books I can never let go: my battered old copy of *The Second Sex*, of course, but also Joseph Campbell's *Hero With a Thousand*

*Faces*; *Writings of the Young Marx on Philosophy and Society*; Aristotle's *Poetics*; Carl Jung's *Four Archetypes* along with *Man and His Symbols*; E. M. W. Tillyard's *The Elizabethan World Picture*; Raymond Williams's *Culture*. Each one of these books opened up a world, sometimes an inner world, sometimes an outer one. Each of them at least gestures toward that simple question, what is the meaning of life?

Back in my university office I surveyed the piles and piles of theory texts. Lacan, Butler, Derrida, Barthes, Bachelard, Irigaray, de Lauretis, Jameson, Foucault, Deleuze and Guattari, Kristeva, Cixous, Mulvey, Althusser, Bourdieu, Spivak. Then I went to work with my scissors. In the flyleaf corner of most of these assiduously collected books I had written my name together with the date and place where I had acquired them. The Museum of Modern Art in New York City; the Bob Miller Book Room in Toronto; Compendium Books in Camden Town in London. A quick snip and that personal history was gone. My boxes and boxes of theory texts were going to the Graduate Student Association book sale and I couldn't bear to imagine younger minds speculating about, and maybe sniggering at, my underlining and marginal notes. All those books, all that effort, boxed and gone.

So why "the turn to theory," as the expression goes? What had I desired from theory? I can't speak for the whole generation of us who made the turn, but I know that what I wanted was context or something like it. My entire undergraduate literary education was based on the close reading practices of New Criticism, though what we did in the classroom and in our assignments was never identified as a particular school or practice. It had become thoroughly naturalized, a transplant from the American South so invasive that our discipline seemed to have forgotten that the landscape had ever looked any different. I value the close-reading skills I acquired as an undergraduate—if nothing else, those skills taught me that what a poem means is less important than how it means. It's the "how it means"—all the images, all the little tricks of creating rhythm—that gets into your bones and your bloodstream.

But a poem (or a novel or a play) doesn't float in free space and it's never inevitable. A thousand decisions that could have been otherwise; a thousand transcriber's or printer's errors; small instances of cowardice or reticence. I longed for the bodies and the stories behind the poems. Bodies at typewriters or moving a quill across scarce parchment. Bodies seeking out wealthy patrons or painstakingly setting their own type and printing their own books or broadsides or pamphlets. Bodies sitting in cafés or drawing rooms or taverns or coffee houses. Bodies rotting in debtors' prison or writing a handful of lines before the children woke up.

But why in the world did I think theory would give me what I was looking for? One simple answer is that theory is what was on offer in North American graduate literature programs in the mid-1970s. It was the emerging alternative to New Criticism. In place of the sternly patriarchal critical judgments of the New Critics, the slipperiness of the French feminist theorists. In place of assertion, critique. In place of the canon, texts. In place of the perfect and isolated poem floating on the white page, the undecidability of language. But if the isolated poem lacked a certain contingency and material thickness so, in the end, did theory. It was exhilarating and often fun, but one was also left with a sense of having talked oneself into a corner from which there was no exit.

I read an early version of this little essay to Stephen. The bastard quoted Ezra Pound to me: "What thou lovest well remains, the rest is dross."

# The Penny Drops

SOMETIMES I THINK SHE WANTS A BETTER relationship with me and then, at other times, she is indifferent or can't be bothered. Something about me annoys her, though, to be fair, the feeling is pretty mutual. I am speaking, of course, about my mother. She is only twenty years older than I am and once, when I was a teenager, I said to her, "We will be old ladies together." I think I meant that we would be old ladies at the same time, but maybe I was even then more hopeful about the possibility of togetherness. Regardless, it is a comment we both remember and now that time has come. We are both old ladies.

I had originally intended to begin this piece like this: "A lot of things fell into place the day I realized that my mother didn't like me. The realization was sudden and immediate, but not in a clap of thunder kind of way. It was more of an... oh. Just oh. Without an exclamation mark, but with a kind of inevitability, as if I'd known it all along, somewhere in the back of my mind. Which I probably had."

So that was my original opening. But then, of course, my mother started being not only a little nicer to me but a little

more outward, a little more self-defining, a little more determined to get something out of her life. I saw her wrestle with
her instinctive irritation and self-pity when one of my sisters,
the sister who struggles with depression and agoraphobia,
didn't show up to a family dinner. I saw her determinedly,
against all her natural inclinations, express appreciation for
a day-long outing to Niagara-on-the-Lake. I thought, "Just
because she's my mother, and just because we're now both
old women, doesn't mean she can't redefine her relationship
to the world." She can be a person with friends; a person who
attends civic meetings opposing new developments; a person
who persuades the other old women in her condo complex to
swarm the local pub on Mondays, seniors' night.

But it is too good an opening to throw away, so I will go
ahead and describe the day I realized that my mother doesn't
like me.

Together with another of my sisters, who also lives out
of town, I was visiting my parents. My father was suffering
from Parkinson's disease and, increasingly, the dementia that
runs, not only in Parkinson's patients, but in his family. This
was a great strain on my mother and so, although I lived
more than thirty-two hundred kilometres away and had a
demanding job, my visits then were more frequent and longer. While I was there I tried to spell her off, to cook meals
that I thought they might like, to stay with my father so that
she could go shopping or play bridge or have lunch with a
friend. I stayed at a nearby motel and never showed up at her
door without something, flowers or pastries or newspapers
or something delicious for dinner. But, except for the flowers,
everything I did was somehow wrong, somehow off-putting.
I was used to this. "Oh, Jo," she would sigh in exasperation
when I painted a damaged floor bright green or installed a

wood burning stove in my suburban living room, actions that offended some ill-defined sense of propriety or property. And yet she delighted in what she saw as the idiosyncrasies of my sister, my fellow out-of-towner: staying single, living in a loft, wearing her hair in a kind of platinum blonde buzz cut, eating breakfast in restaurants most mornings.

On this particular night, I had cooked dinner for the four of us. Afterwards my father retreated to the den to watch the baseball game. My mother and sister sat on at the dining room table, their conversation apparently confiding and intense, while I cleared and washed up. I watched them briefly from the doorway and that's when the penny dropped. Oh, I thought. Well, that explains everything. But not only was the realization that my mother doesn't like me not upsetting, it was as if a weight lifted from my shoulders. I felt, curiously, absolved. I had no doubt that she loved me; she just didn't particularly like me. In a telephone conversation not long after, we were talking about my aunt, her sister. My aunt and her second husband lived in a luxurious assisted living centre, paid for by one of her four children. My mother commented with some amusement that my aunt always complained about this son. "He's never been her favourite," my mother said, as if this was an acceptable thing to say.

I think back on my life, my long and usually unsuccessful struggle against propriety. I think about my first marriage, the husband I gave my parents like a kind of gift. Handsome, ambitious, sporting, an MBA when MBAs were still shiny and new. I think about my profession, about how being an English professor was the furthest my rope could stretch towards the unconventional. I think about my first year living on my own. For Christmas, I asked my mother for a good pair of scissors and *The Joy of Cooking*. She gave me a tiny six-inch pair of scissors and volume two of the paperback edition of the cookbook. Volume two was appetizers, desserts, and baked goods. All the main courses were in volume one. What was she trying to tell me? That I was wrong to try to cut the tie, to be a young single woman living alone, to nourish myself? I think further back to my childhood, to her depressions and "bad moods," as I described them then. The oldest of four girls, I would creep out of my bedroom to make bright conversation until her mood lightened. Back then, I was the great mollifier.

Why rehearse all of this now, when we are both old women? In an essay published in *Slouching towards Bethlehem*, Joan Didion describes one of her memories as "a home movie run all too often." She wonders whether the memory is true or not. She wonders whether it matters if it's true. What really matters, she thinks, is *how it felt to me*. And, more recently, Deborah Levy has observed that "to speak our life as we feel it is a freedom we mostly choose not to take." This is what I hold on to now. What matters is how it feels to me and what I do with it, and what I want to do with it is let it go.

A few months ago, I made a new and unexpected friend, someone I don't see nearly often enough. She is almost the same age as my mother and, like my mother, she had four children in seven years, beginning when she was twenty. Unlike my mother, she had a dream, a literal dream, that, if she stayed home, she would murder her children by throwing them off the top of a mountain. She went back to school, took an advanced degree, became pre-eminent in her profession. She is sophisticated, charming, warm. On the surface, at least, she couldn't be less like my mother. But, looking back, she worries at the beads of her life. Was she a cold mother? Does her oldest have problems because she didn't cuddle him

enough when he was a baby? I get the sense she is slightly suspicious of her oldest, but wishes him well. I tell her a
brief story about the radio always being on in our house, my
mother's constant companion. I describe how she would pass
along the radio gossip about Rock Hudson or Bobby Darin.
My friend wants my story to be longer and warmer, but that's
all I've got.

Why doesn't my mother like me? I think it's probably no
more complicated than chalk and cheese. I'm a lot more like
my father than I am like her. I'm the only one in my family
to have his dark brown eyes. I am not confiding, and I don't
share her family's gift of easy gab. When I brought my friends
home, it was not to sit around her kitchen table, as my younger sisters did with their friends, but to retreat to my bedroom
or the rec room. And—somewhat to my own surprise, since
I see this only retrospectively—I seem to have inherited the
Wallace self-confidence. My mother's unease about her class
background and lack of education (she didn't go past grade
nine) has often made it difficult for her to feel fully comfortable in the life she and my father attained.

Since his death, it has become clear to me that, for her,
it was not a particularly happy marriage, at least not in the
later years... decades? When I was little, they would sit in
the kitchen after all the kids had gone to bed. Sometimes
his feet would be in her lap, and she would stroke his leg as
they quietly talked about the day. I would sneak out of my
room and see this. The move from inner-city Montreal to a
middle-class suburb wasn't, at first, easy for her. No buses
or streetcars or corner stores. No hustle and bustle. Their
move, years later, to a slightly tonier Toronto suburb, where
her next-door neighbour was a member of the United Empire
Loyalists (the neighbour let this nugget drop pretty early

in their relationship), was perhaps even more difficult. My father's new job required extensive international travel, and my mother resented what she perceived as his abandonment of her.

So, in the end, she didn't very much like him either though she may once have loved him. And this, I guess, is the crux of the matter. I am tempted to write that loving each other is more important than liking each other, but that, in the language of my youth, would be a cop out. Liking implies separateness, difference. You're over there and I'm over here, and yet I take an interest. I am curious, I want to know more. I think I would rather my mother liked me, but instead I must settle for her love and she must settle for mine.

I am listening to a friend talk to her elderly father on the phone. He has been to a neighbour's for supper. "What did Florence cook?" my friend asks. Fish, her father answers. What kind of fish? "Oh, you know, President's Choice frozen fish. She cooked it in the oven." I am unreasonably charmed by this exchange, the generic fish, the generic cooking method. I know this is the way forward and that, as so often in life, it is the merely sufficient that suffices.

# Iceland

I RECENTLY BOUGHT A SET OF RUNES, CASTING stones inscribed with the ancient Germanic alphabet that dates from round 150 AD. My runes are made of blue quartz and I knitted them a bag made of rough Icelandic wool, which seemed appropriate given their association, in the popular imagination at least, with Vikings. Why did I buy runes? I pride myself on my commitment to reason, on being a rational person, and yet.... And yet buying the runes satisfied a long-held desire which I have difficulty articulating. It is not a desire to pull back the curtain or veil. It's more like a desire to think *into* things, first and last things, the kind of things a religious person might seek from the church or scripture. But I tried church and it just felt like a really crappy and badly run department meeting. Thus the runes.

I am not "casting" them, either for myself or for others. But most days I draw one and consult various sources about the significance of that particular rune. Oddly—or is it odd?—I tend to draw the same runes over and over. Ehwaz and Gebo especially, but also Berkana and Algiz. Gebo kind of freaks me out, maybe because it's shaped like an X, like something being crossed out, though apparently it is better understood as a rune of exchange, gift giving, and obligation. One source, though, calls it "the rune of spiritual and emotional challenges, of the spiritual descent." She goes on to say that "Sacrifice is involved in Gebo. Blood is involved in Gebo. It ties into Odin on the tree: mystical, sacred shamanic sacrifice and the resulting awareness." Well, okay then.

A reader might wonder if I "believe in" the runes, but I think that's the wrong question. Obviously, I don't think they have any ability to divine the future. (And isn't it interesting that divine is both a noun and a verb?) But they are an occasion to think into things and to ask oneself questions, like "am I paying sufficient attention to what is happening to me now?" And they seem to be influencing my dreams which, these days, are long, narratively complex, and full of journeys of one kind or another.

Knitting the rune bag and handling its rough Icelandic yarn made me think a lot about one particular journey, a journey that hasn't yet made it into my dreams, at least not in any overt way. In early autumn 2014, the year I took a buyout and early retirement, I flew to Iceland for a two-week tour of the island with two women colleagues, Denise and Deirdre, both of whom had also taken the buyout. Iceland seemed the perfect place to consider the next stage of our lives. It is a land in seemingly endless formation, steaming and spewing, the activity of its volcanos constantly creating new black lava fields, plate tectonics expanding some of its smaller islands. In a way, it's what we wanted for ourselves, an unconstrained and fiery new life.

In Edmonton, together with Denise, I boarded the tightly packed and highly confined Icelandair direct flight to Reykjavík. Deirdre, who was attending a conference in

Norway, would meet us there. Most of the passengers were backpackers, quite a bit younger than I, and they quickly settled into their earbuds and home-packed dinners. I tried to sleep. Six or seven hours later we disgorged at the small Reykjavík airport where I checked my email for the first time since leaving Edmonton. There was a note from my mother telling me that my father had died. He must have died while I was somewhere over Hudson Bay or Baffin Bay or maybe Greenland. I imagined us passing like the proverbial two ships in the night, my father heading off to who-knows-where, me on my way to one of the most volatile land masses on earth.

What was to be done? I couldn't bear to talk to my mother, so I telephoned my husband, Stephen. He took on the task of calling her and conveying information back and forth between us. While this was going on, and while Denise and I were waiting for Deirdre's flight to arrive from Norway, I walked across the airport and booked the next direct flight back to Edmonton. The next direct flight would be three days later, information that Stephen delivered to my mother in Oakville. She was concerned that my father's funeral service not conflict with her bridge club meeting because she wanted to ensure a decent rollout at the funeral and knew she could count on the ladies.

Why didn't I want to talk to my mother? I was distressed that she hadn't told me that my father was close to death. Is it unfair or cruel to say that she regards illness and death as faux pas? Cruel maybe, but not altogether unfair. She found it unsurprisingly difficult when dementia was added to the challenges presented by my father's Parkinson's disease. Sundowning syndrome meant that he became agitated in the evening, restless and anxious for something to do, some way to assert or express himself. He would want to take mechanical things apart, apparently imagining that he was repairing them. A local choirmaster lived down the hall in my parents' condominium complex and one evening my father knocked on his door, saying that he wanted to sing in the choir and requesting an audition. The choirmaster, knowing my father's condition, admitted him and listened to him sing. My mother was mortified and, instead of thanking the choirmaster for his kindness, apologized profusely for my father's behaviour. When my father was finally admitted to a long-term care home, singing with the group was the one thing that seemed to console him, but my mother was embarrassed by the rapt expression on his face. One of my sisters wanted to give him a fuzzy, red heart-shaped pillow because she had read that dementia sufferers find it comforting to have something soft to hold onto, but my mother wouldn't let her present it to him. It would be embarrassing for a man to have such a thing in his possession.

Am I being unfair? Am I being cruel? It is true that my mother bore an intolerable burden when my father still lived at home. It is true that she visited him every day when he was in the care home. But did she visit him because she loved him, or loved the man he once was, or because she wanted to be seen to be doing the right thing? Because it is also true that, to this day, the only stories she tells about him are about the ways he frustrated or embarrassed her in his final years. I have not heard her say a single affectionate thing about the man, my father, to whom she was married for sixty-two years in what I had, until his decline, imagined was a reasonably loving marriage.

I didn't talk to my mother until I arrived in Oakville for the memorial service. I spent the three days in Reykjavík, flew back to Edmonton, spent a couple of days there, using that time to write my father's eulogy, and then flew to Ontario. I didn't even know whether my father had been cremated or whether there would be a coffin. At the funeral home I spotted a shiny wooden box. "Is that him?" I asked one of my sisters.

The occasion was a success. The bridge club came. My oldest friend arrived from Montreal, bringing with her one of my former boyfriends, and that pleased my mother. My youngest sister's employer came, also pleasing. The choirmaster told my mother that he was impressed by my PhD and my career, and my mother liked that. People admired my eulogy, and she liked that too.

What did I do during my three days in Reykjavík? On the first day, Denise and Deirdre headed off to take a tour down the throat of a volcano. I stayed back. I walked downtown and had coffee at a bookstore. I wandered around trying to find somewhere to buy Kleenex, among other things, and eventually found myself at Bónus, the Icelandic chain of discount stores. Bónus is known for the bright pink cartoon pig that serves as its logo and I was pleased to walk away with a plastic shopping bag featuring the pig. My stepdaughter had given away the piggy bags she acquired during her visit to Iceland, and she badly wanted another.

I made my way to the massive Hallgrimskirkja church, easy to find since its towering brutalist spire and jagged facade dominate the Reykjavík skyline. The church interior is massive and stark white. I sat in one of the pews and wept as groups of tourists walked by. I imagined them thinking, "Look at that poor Icelandic woman with her pink pig shopping bag. Why is she crying?"

In the evenings, Denise, Deirdre, and I drank red wine and ate the enormous Toblerone chocolate bar that Deirdre had brought from Norway. One morning I left early and alone to buy bread and croissants at the local bakery, and to watch the pointy-nosed, serious denizens of Reykjavík making their way to work. We were given a tour of Reykjavík University by a former University of Alberta graduate student, where we admired an installation of flying Canada geese in recognition of the financial contributions made by Manitobans of Icelandic descent. We visited The Pearl, the museum and rotating glass dome that also serves as a water reservoir for the city. We visited Harpen, the stunning concert hall, its glass facade echoing the crystallized basalt columns of Iceland.

And then I left. Denise and Deirdre drove me to the airport, the road leading along the edge of the North American tectonic plate where it meets the Eurasian plate, through endless fields of spiky, black volcanic rock. An inhospitable but compelling landscape.

And what about my mother? Of the three girls in her family, she made the best marriage. One of her sisters married a welder who had suffered a mild brain injury. He was a kind man and my aunt loved him unreservedly. Her other sister married a man who quickly became paranoid, abusive, a hoarder. My father was ambitious and disciplined and he eventually became vice president of a large, international insurance brokerage, where he specialized in assessing petrochemical corporations. He toured facilities in places as diverse as northern Ontario and Belize, later blaming his exposure to volatile chemicals for his Parkinson's. When he moved to a Toronto brokerage, after I had already left home, he and my mother joined a prestigious golf club. They dined out often. My mother liked the fact that he was well dressed and tall. On social occasions she would tuck her head into his shoulder and look up at him flirtatiously. But did she love him?

Who knows? I don't.

I do know that after a couple of years of complaining about eating alone, she bravely made a good life for herself, expanding her network of friends, driving the other old ladies to the pub for dinner on seniors' night, enjoying her bridge club. She weathered the pandemic with unexpected good humour and grace. Those may have been her best years.

● ● ●

A handful of years have passed since I wrote this piece, and my mother is now very old indeed. Decades of heavy smoking, given up only when her second grandchild was born, mean that she is on oxygen support. She gave up driving shortly before she turned ninety. My sisters tell me that she is very insistent about one thing. If one of us is on holiday when she dies, her death must be kept a secret until the holiday is over. I know this is her way of being kind, of not making a fuss, of treating death as an inconvenience. But that was never the point.

# Patina

MY MOTHER IS UNDERTAKING HER OWN VERSION of Swedish death cleaning, even though she's been an inveterate thrower-out of things as long as I can remember. There's really not that much to get rid of. But she's at it again, rummaging through drawers and fretting over the items that have accumulated in her not very crowded condo storage locker in southern Ontario. Her recent excavations unearthed a couple of drawings made by four-year-old me, a 1953 silver dollar that was a gift from her father to newly born me, and a handwritten document from her maternal grandmother to "all concerned in the Family." It's an odd contract of sorts, written in a kind of legalese that my great-grandmother must have picked up from somewhere. It reads as follows:

> This letter to all concerned in the Family of the late John Gerrard Neale late of 402 St. Antoine St Lachine Que. All the Brass now in use, namely brass Trays, Candlesticks etc. & especially the Fireplace Fixtures, as Fender and Fireirons, which are at present in the care of Mrs. Thos. Pape [?], Ada Neale, Daughter of

the late J. G. Neale. They are to be regarded as Heir Looms. In the Event of the death of the said Mrs Thos Pape the Brass to be returned to the children or relatives as Heirlooms in the Family & are definitely not to be sold or given away. Signed, my name Mrs Christina Neale, widow of the late John G. Neale of Lachine. Witness my hand this day, 11TH day of September 1945.

My mother eventually inherited a lot of this brass from her Aunt Ada. In addition to the fireplace fender and fire irons mentioned in my great-grandmother's instructions, she has brass trays, a heavy brass floor lamp, a magnificent brass sculpture of the legendary racehorse Man o' War, and a large vase made from a brass artillery shell. My childhood memories are punctuated by the smell of Brasso—those many Heir Looms, to use my great-grandmother's insistent phrase, requiring frequent polishing.

The brass is all the product of the venerable Robert Mitchell Company brass works, established in Montreal in 1851 and still active in St. Laurent. Its founder, a young Scottish immigrant, had arrived only three years earlier, penniless because a fire in the river steamer that carried him upriver from the port of Quebec City had burned through the hold in no time, destroying everything that the new settlers had brought with them. Ironically, it was another fire—the Great Fire of July 1852, which destroyed more than eleven thousand businesses and residences—that ensured the success of the newly founded Mitchell brass works, first located in a shed on Rue Henri. In response to the two defining catastrophes of his still short life, Robert Mitchell designed an improved brass fire hose coupling and nozzle, featured at the 1855

Paris Exhibition. They were still being sold across the country seventy years later. The extension of the Grand Trunk line between Montreal and Toronto offered further opportunities for expansion, and Mitchell moved into manufacturing brass fittings for railway cars. Mitchell products—sanitary fixtures, architectural bronze work, iron staircases, revolving doors— eventually found their way to every prestigious Canadian institution, from the Senate Chamber in Ottawa to the Banff Springs Hotel in Alberta.

My great-grandfather, John Gerrard Neale, worked at the Robert Mitchell Company, and his position was clearly a source of pride for the family. It's not altogether clear what he did there, but my mother remembers that he wore what she calls "office clothes." These signalled what she describes as a "better class" of people than those on the paternal side of her family, all of them descended from carpenters, domestics, and grooms. John, on the other hand, apparently "came from money in England." The United Kingdom's 1881 census indicates that his father, my great-great-grandfather, was a "tobacconist and stationer," putting the family, I guess, in the petit bourgeois echelon. Regardless, John and his younger brother were shipped off to Canada from Liverpool, apparently because they were "into something" their father disapproved of.

My great-grandfather carried his own father's social aspirations with him to the new country, acquiring a solid two-story brick house in Lachine, only four blocks from the convent where he insisted that his Protestant daughters be educated. He wanted them to be ladies. His third daughter, Doris, my grandmother, foiled at least some of his ambitions by cutting classes and marrying a sometimes self-employed, but mostly unemployed, carpenter. No wonder her older sister Ada got the family brass, which, nonetheless, found its way to my mother sometime in the 1960s.

In one of our recent conversations about the brass, my mother—clearly willing to disregard her grandmother's insistence that the brass pieces all be treated as Heir Looms in perpetuity—suggested that the heavy floor lamp might be sold for a good price. It was originally designed to hold candles, and the four lions' feet on the base have holes in them so that the whole thing could be screwed to a wooden floor. When my great-grandparents had electricity installed in their home, the lamp was converted to accommodate light bulbs.

I didn't have the heart to tell my mother that, some years earlier, she had pretty much sabotaged its value on the antiques market. A piece of the lamp had somehow broken off and, when my parents had it fixed, the repairman suggested they have it coated with a sealer, probably polyurethane. This would preserve a bright, polished surface. Uh oh. It would also, of course, completely ruin the patina—that now much valued symbol of an artifact's or work of art's provenance and authenticity. Today, silver candlesticks must show traces of tarnish, wooden tables must have deepened in colour and perhaps accumulated a few dings. Alas, my mother's brass floor lamp now shines with a permanent and preternatural brightness that it never had before the repairman "improved" it.

It would never have occurred to my mother, or her ancestors (a word she never uses), that any kind of tarnish or discoloration could be a good thing. On the contrary, respectability demanded that brass and silver be polished to a high sheen. It went without saying that furniture or doors with layers of varicoloured chipped paint should be repainted. Nowadays, of course, even the most culturally naive among us values the look of age and authenticity, whether genuine or not.

The internet is replete with advice about how to add patina to almost anything. "Adding patina to silver with an egg." "How to age brass using vinegar and salt." "How to make your wood furniture look distressed." Martha Stewart, the doyenne of all things domestic and a great popularizer of the desirability of patina, even has articles on how to add algae and moss and other signs of age to one's terracotta garden pots. You can slather yoghurt on the pot, she explains. You can fill it with a highly concentrated fertilizer solution for a few weeks. To make a new planter look as if it had been unearthed in an archaeological dig, you can apply soil from your backyard. Of course, my mother would simply consider the result to be a dirty pot. The long-running television program *Antiques Roadshow* has been another great popularizer of the significance of patina, with its parade of disappointed hopefuls learning that their Tiffany lamp has declined in value from $50,000 to $10,000 because they cleaned the bronze base.

But let's assume that the patina on an object, on a collectible—a terracotta pot, a wooden table, a brass lamp—is real, an effect of the passage of time, the accumulation of dirt, various chemical reactions, natural weathering. The passage of time works its effects impersonally, without agency. What we don't see when we focus on the patina of an object is labour and pride of labour. The labour of working at a forge or in a carpenter's workshop. The labour of keeping a clean and well-run house. The labour of preserving and repairing a useful object when objects were not so easily acquired or replaced. The word *heirloom* gestures to this labour, with loom meaning "tool" or "utensil." An heirloom was something useful or necessary passed down through the family.

The word patina also evokes the work of a household. It comes from the Italian word with the same meaning as in

English, and, before that, from Latin, where it refers to a "broad shallow dish or pan" and the "prepared food contained in such a dish." The *Oxford English Dictionary* conjectures that its current English and Italian meaning derives from the film that would form on such a copper pan or dish after prolonged use. But we have lost this old emphasis on use and entered into a commodification of the heirloom. It is only when the heirloom leaves the family that it accrues the monetary value so celebrated by *Antiques Roadshow*—and, may I add, by my mother, a child of the Depression. For her, things are marked in the first instance by their exchange value. Not long ago on the phone, for instance, I told her that my husband had finally located his treasured hockey card collection, which he feared he had lost in our recent move from Edmonton to Victoria. It consists of fifteen signed cards from many of the 1962–63 Toronto Maple Leafs, lovingly mounted in a photo album. He wrote to each of them—Johnny Bower, Red Kelly, Tim Horton, and the others— individually from a childhood sickbed. "You are my favourite Leaf," he maintained faithlessly. "Please send me a signed card." And they arrived, as if by magic, by return mail. "He could probably get a good price for them" was my mother's response.

My mother has made a terrible and heartbreaking mistake in one way, by removing even the possibility that her brass floor lamp can now acquire patina. But in another way, she has been the honest keeper of a trust, maintaining the usefulness of a lamp that started its life in the age of the candle. My sisters will make sure all the brass stays in the family, as my great-grandmother stipulated almost eighty years ago. But none of it will come to me, not least because my mother would consider it a terrible waste of money to ship something all the way across the country when another perfectly adequate child lives only a few kilometers away.

# Cancer in the Time of COVID
## (Summer 2022)

IT HAD BEEN A WHILE SINCE WE'D HAD A FAMILY doctor and when we finally secured one, she sent us for the usual battery of tests. My FIT test rang a bell with BC Cancer and I was scheduled for a colonoscopy. I was relatively unworried. We're a heart-and-stroke kind of family, I thought, not a cancer family. The doctor and nurses were all pretty jolly as the procedure began, but very soon the temperature in the room dropped noticeably. No one would meet my eyes as I was wheeled out.

COVID restrictions meant that (with some exceptions for clients who spoke no English or had severe mobility issues) we were not permitted to have family members or other support people accompany us in the colonoscopy clinic. It was another sign of the seriousness of my situation that my husband was invited to join me when the resident surgeon came out to deliver the bad news. An MRI later, the news would only get worse. Colorectal cancer. Not the most glamourous of cancers, I remember thinking.

The initial meeting with my oncologist took place, not in his office, but in an examination room at the cancer agency.

This must have been to accommodate the mandated space between the three of us. Even my husband and I were seated the requisite two metres apart. We were all masked. The oncologist delivered the news kindly but firmly. Stage IV. Cancer spread to my liver and lungs. Not curable but it was treatable, the treatment aimed at quality of life.

The life expectancy for people with my type and stage of cancer, he said, is one to two years.

In the twenty months since my diagnosis, this is the only in-person meeting I have had with my oncologist. Since COVID, telephone consultations have become the new norm.

I began chemotherapy on January 4, 2021, anticipating that I would undergo six treatment cycles over the course of twelve weeks. Two days later, still feeling pretty lousy, I sat in my reading chair and watched as the mob stormed Congress. It felt like a metaphor.

It was a bit of a shock to realize, later, that my chemotherapy—they call it "chemo-lite" or "maintenance chemo"—will extend as long as I can tolerate it or as long as it keeps the cancer at bay. I'm now twenty months into it. All of my symptoms now are the side effects of the toxic chemicals that have been moving through my body.

Cancer treatment has become massively standardized and it can be hard not to feel that one is a widget on a rolling conveyer belt. CT scan every three months. Telephone consultation with oncologist every three months. Nurse practitioner consultations every four weeks. Chemo treatment every two. The only people I see in person are the cancer nurses. When I began treatment, at the height of the COVID epidemic, they wore masks and plastic visors over their faces, plastic coveralls over their scrubs, and they said it was like being in a sauna, for hours. I have never seen their faces, even now, when they are down to one mask and paper coveralls. They have never seen mine. It surprises and pains me to realize that still, only two or three of the nurses recognize me enough to say a casual hello as they pass in the treatment room.

In spite of these necessary but alienating precautions, we are all unfailingly courteous with one another and the atmosphere in the treatment room is quiet and calm. Once in a blue moon something unusual happens, like the time I was seated next to a cheerful man in his late middle-age, plugged into his iPhone and loudly singing along to country-and-western songs, all in the "she done me wrong" mode.

For a long time, we cancer patients were on our own. There were no visitors and our chairs were positioned far apart from one another. A few weeks ago, we were once again permitted to bring companions into the treatment room but hardly any of us have done so. Mostly we prefer to read our books, do our crossword puzzles, check our devices, and doze. We don't feel compelled to have cheerful conversations. We don't want to play hostess, not even with one another. The nurses tell me this is a change, one they like.

I understand that in the pre-COVID "before times", the atmosphere in the treatment room was different. There were volunteers with tea trolleys and therapy dogs. A coffee shop. A wig-and-hat shop catering to patients who were losing their hair. More visitors and companions. Meeting rooms for support groups and on-site psychologists. Now there are greeters at the door who quiz us about COVID symptoms and ensure that we sanitize our hands and wear new masks as we enter the building.

But here's what I have to ask myself. Is it better like this? Scaled down, scaled back. No pressure to join support groups or take up yoga or meditation for people "living with cancer."

No pressure to see a psychologist or to tick items off my bucket list. Cancer has made me realize that my ordinary, daily life is my bucket list. Taking the dog for walks, tending the garden, reading and writing, cracking jokes and watching TV with my husband. For me, at least, having cancer in the time of COVID, when there are fewer possibilities and therefore fewer expectations, takes a lot of the weight off.

Something else that takes the weight off is Canada's Medical Assistance in Dying (MAiD) law. I can't imagine going through this without that consolation. The great inconsolable, of course, is the thought of leaving my husband alone, but in that I have to trust in his inherent strength.

And I have developed a handful of mantras that help me negotiate this period in my life. Take one day at a time. Practice equanimity. Live neither in hope nor despair. Live as if I'm going to live while accepting that I'm not. This means, among other things, planting bulbs in the fall. Cancer in the time of COVID has freed me to live my ordinary life, not heroically, not engaged in a courageous battle: just living. After all, I'm alive until I'm not.

# The Women's Ward

*I AM ANCHORED TO THE BED. A CATHETER DRAINS into a plastic jug on the floor. A saline solution and painkillers drip into my arm through intravenous tubes. Young women come and go, measuring my blood pressure, my oxygen levels, my temperature. I lie on my back, unmoving. The drugs do their work and the situation is not unpleasant. I listen, locating myself. How many of us are there? Who are we? What is this country in which we find ourselves?*

## Doreen

DOREEN LIES ACROSS FROM ME. SHE IS ANCIENT, her body marble white, wispy, barely there. Eventually, I make my way to the bathroom and peek into the curtained alcove where she is sleeping, curled up in the bed like a tiny, bald, newly hatched bird. A garrulous hatchling, as I discover, a chattering magpie, her feathery yet penetrating old-woman's voice alternately querulous, demanding, grateful, intimate. When there is no one to talk to—the nurses and aid workers must eventually walk away—she talks to herself. Now she is whimpering, distressed. She wants a bedpan, but the nurse is reluctant to bring one because Doreen has found them too difficult to use. "Go in your briefs," the nurse keeps saying and Doreen keeps refusing. Eventually she loses control. Her tone changes from the imperious to the abject; she feels badly that the nurse must clean and change her. And yet, a day later, a handsome Hispanic nurse shows up at her bedside and she is charmed. "Oh, a man," she says, and is happy to be cleaned and changed by him.

Doreen has a rented television which she plays loudly and unceasingly. The nurses persuade her to turn the volume down a bit at night, but I can still hear it. She is particularly attached to American serial dramas like *CSI: Crime Scene Investigation* and I am reminded how awful they are, the women invariably beautiful, their voices always weirdly modulated. In the middle of the night, I consider asking the nurse to turn the volume off, but then I remember the comfort Doreen draws from the incessant prattle, the simulacrum of life.

Doreen's daughter comes to see her every day after work, a one-hour drive through bad weather. She brings food: croissants, a bit of steak, all manner of delicacies. But she does it resentfully. "What did you have for supper?" Doreen asks. "Supper?" the daughter replies. "I drive here right after work. I haven't cooked for myself in days." The daughter's resentment—which feels to me, lying on the other side of the room, like barely controlled fury—washes over Doreen, who continues to chatter away. Eventually the daughter's ruffled feathers smooth and they watch television almost companionably. Other visitors arrive and leave. A young man who loves gossip as much as Doreen. An older couple with the feel of church people. A friend telephones, bellowing through the speaker on Doreen's phone, crude and aggressive. Is everyone in Doreen's world perpetually pissed off? An aid worker drops by with the gift of conversation, Doreen's most cherished commodity. "What kind of work did you do?" the aid worker asks. Doreen says she was a bouncer at the local Legion. "A little thing like you?" says the aid worker and Doreen cackles happily in response.

# Joan

THE BED NEXT TO DOREEN IS OCCUPIED BY JOAN who, judging solely by her voice, strikes me as a quiet, dignified, older woman. Her bed is one of two beside a large window that overlooks the parking lot and, beyond it, trees, and the promise of green life. At first the view is a mystery to me. The curtains between our beds remain permanently drawn and I have no access to the window and the world it intimates. Even after I am released from the catheter that, for the first twenty-four hours, chained me to my bed, even after I have been encouraged to take short walks, I have no credible excuse to wander past Joan, to look out the window or to have a peek at her. And so, I construct an image based on her calm, slightly passive voice. I imagine a lady (the word seems apt) with short grey hair worn in the loose curls that many older women, like the late Queen Elizabeth, favour.

Like Doreen, Joan has rented a television, though hers remains tuned to a news channel and she turns it off at night. She reads a newspaper all day long. Based on the speed and regularity of the turning pages, I think she must read everything, top to bottom. The turning pages sound soft, like paper that has sat in a damp environment or been repeatedly folded. A nurse asks if she can remove the used newspaper.

"No," Joan says, a little panicked, and I realize then that she has been reading the same newspaper, the same stories, over and over again.

Joan's husband comes to see her every afternoon. He is profoundly deaf with a loud, gruff voice. Joan uncomplainingly repeats everything two or three times, seeming not to mind. I have the impression they love each other very much. Then I catch a glimpse of the husband as he leaves and, to my astonishment, he has a ponytail. A thin, grey, unattractive ponytail at the base of his skull. This is not the appearance of a man married to a woman with Queen Elizabeth's hair. I realize I must reimagine Joan.

After a couple of days, Joan is strong enough to be wheeled to the bathroom on the other side of my bed and to be enthroned on a high commode. As she makes her stately way past, I see that straight grey hair hangs halfway down her back and that her face has a quality Robertson Davies once described as being like a pan of milk. I begin to wonder if Joan is perhaps a bit simple. Maybe she has indulged a little too much in that old hippy lettuce, Mary Jane, ganja, weed. Because it is suddenly clear to me that Joan and her husband are a couple of ancient hippies.

Finally, there is much commotion around Joan's bed. She is going home, and arrangements must be made, pulleys and wheelchairs and commodes and contraptions of all kinds must be procured. As she leaves, attended by the EMS workers who will take her the one-hour drive to the hippy haven of Sooke, she bestows on me a small, wordless smile.

# Lucia

IN THE BED BESIDE MINE AND ACROSS FROM Joan's is Lucia. Like Joan, she has the window, but she refuses the view, refuses the sunrise, insists that her curtain remain drawn. "You don't want to see the run rise?" asks an aid worker, incredulously, as she brings us all fresh ice water. "No." Lucia refuses everything. She is depressed, sullen, and suspicious. She is also hugely nauseous, throwing up repeatedly but refusing to take an anti-nausea pill. She speaks reluctantly, in a low, heavily accented mumble that makes it difficult for the nurses to untangle what she is saying. Her voice is so low that, even though we are separated by no more than three or four feet, it takes me a while to understand that her first language is German. I hear the nurses refer to her colostomy bag, but it is unclear to me whether it is a new development or something she has lived with for a while. An aid worker does a circuit of all four of our beds with her electronic tablet, recording what we would like for our lunch and dinner. Lucia refuses to eat and insists on nothing more than room-temperature tap water. A little soup? Some milk or juice? No, no. She rings her call bell frequently and asks that her pillows be rearranged, but that is the only concession she will make to her comfort.

Her refusal of food, of medicine, of sunrises makes me think she is willing herself to die. My suspicion appears to be confirmed when discharge workers start showing up at her bedside, pressing her to make plans for her release. She needs twenty-four-hour care. This means three carers, each working an eight-hour shift. What happens if one of the care workers doesn't show up? Is there anyone in the trailer park she can call on? A professional has already been to her home to assess it. Does the shower work? Why is the shower full of clothes? Now I think Lucia might be a hoarder, or at the very least an appalling slob, and I feel pain on her behalf. The indignity of being the object of professional scrutiny and judgment.

The discharge nurses—or are they social workers?—finally raise the question they have been working toward all along. Has Lucia considered going into hospice? She would have her own room and excellent care. No, no. Finally, Lucia nerves herself to ask the question that must have been tormenting her. "How much?" "It's free," says the discharge worker. "It's like the hospital. The government pays for it." The relief on the other side of the curtain is palpable.

The discharge workers have made repeated references to "Walter," and finally Walter and a brisk younger woman show up. It becomes clear that he is Lucia's brother and the younger woman, who is probably in her late thirties, is her niece. Walter will assume power of attorney but he hastily, and almost tearfully, assures Lucia that "I won't do anything you don't want." "What will happen to my trailer?" Lucia asks. The niece tells a long and improbable story about a young man in her town who became a paraplegic as the result of a skiing accident and somehow went on to become a quadriplegic following a hiking accident. Is this supposed to make Lucia feel better, or maybe even lucky? "It was nice to meet you," says the niece to Lucia as she leaves, trailing a definite scent of patchouli behind her.

*I KNOW THAT FEELING, THE NIECE'S FEELING, AS, having done her duty, she leaves the women's ward. Feeling alive, healthy, strong. Feeling relief. Leaving my grandmother behind, leaving my father behind, throwing open the door and striding out into the green world beyond the window, taking a deep breath. The women's ward is the other side of the looking glass, a day for night world, never really dark and never really light. Joan has left and been replaced. I will leave tomorrow or the day after. Lucia will leave when a place has been secured for her at a hospice. Doreen seems set to stay.*

# We Have No Chicken Today

ONE OF THE UNANTICIPATED COMPENSATIONS OF a cancer diagnosis, particularly a diagnosis of advanced cancer, is that you feel old animosities melting away. Rapprochements are achieved, as old friends, and sometimes old rivals, hear the news. People reach out and are kind. I feel loved and I am grateful for that feeling.

One of the people who reached out to me was a colleague from grad school who ended up with a tenured position in the same English department as I did. Jacqui and I had always had a tangled relationship. We were both young, both feminists, and we had the same initials. People constantly mistook us for one another which was hilarious because we couldn't have been more different. I was the careful one, the one who assumed administrative responsibilities and became more familiar with *Robert's Rules of Order* than I could ever have imagined. Jacqui was the firebrand: the one who stood on her head at department parties, who loudly denounced every form of injustice, who wreaked havoc in the classroom but also inspired great affection in some of her students. On the odd occasion when I did something just a little outlandish, like anonymously producing and distributing a satirical one-page newspaper poking fun at the Merit Only group, a group of professors that organized to oppose the hiring of five women by my department, the action was attributed to Jacqui. Even now, after I have numerous times confessed to being the author of the little newspaper, people still remember it as Jacqui's exploit.

But Jacqui reached out, and because she did, I was re-connected, via a three-way Messenger post that she initiated, with another friend from grad school, Kim Echlin. Unlike Jacqui and me, Kim veered away from the academic life, instead becoming a producer for CBC's *As It Happens* while Barbara Frum was still alive. When she left, it was to devote herself to her writing, and she eventually published several very well-received novels. Kim and I co-taught a course at York University the summer before I moved to Edmonton, and that summer we also—for reasons I cannot reconstruct—visited various soothsayers in Toronto: tarot card readers, rune readers, palm readers, a man who professed to read our auras, etc., etc. As we were driving to or from one of these odd forays, Kim taught me how to remove my bra without removing my top, perhaps the most useful lesson of my graduate student days.

In one of our online exchanges, Kim asked me what I remembered about graduate school, saying that she herself remembered it as "such a kind of disconnected period in my life." I told her that I, too, remembered it as a disconnected, even disjointed, time. Much of this had to do with my personal life. During those years I moved several times, living in Toronto, then Port Dover (a small fishing town on the north shore of Lake Erie), then Hamilton, then Toronto again. I married, we bought a house, I tried to get pregnant and couldn't. My marriage fell apart when my husband began an affair while I was in the hospital having a tuboplasty, an operation to open up my blocked fallopian tubes. He couldn't bear the thought of not having biological children of his own, but his Irish Catholic upbringing also meant he couldn't bear the guilt of being unfaithful. The result was a handful of years of dangerously self-destructive behaviour on his part—including a six-month driver's license suspension for drunk driving. This coincided with what can only be described as a form of unintentionally cruel gaslighting, leading me to believe our marriage might be salvaged while he carried on with his new relationship. Some devious googling tells me that he and his new wife went on to have four children.

The moves to Port Dover and then Hamilton had been to accommodate his career. My long commutes from each of those communities to teach in Toronto—often more than two hours from Port Dover, effectively driving from one Great Lake to another—made it impossible to complete my dissertation in a timely way, as did the isolation from any academic community. Two or three times a week, I would leave very early in the morning, in the dark, before six o'clock in the morning. As I drove down Main Street, I would see women walking down to the port to begin the work of packing the previous day's catch, mostly smelt intended for the Japanese market. That was Port Dover's claim to fame: "the world's largest exporter of smelt to Japan." The commute from Hamilton was half the distance, but all of it was on knuckle-whitening major highways, the 427, the QEW, the 401. When I got home in the afternoon I would watch *The Guiding Light*, a long-running soap opera to which I found myself strangely addicted. At night I dreamed about the characters as if they were my friends.

When my husband and I separated, I moved back to Toronto but to a much tighter and more difficult rental market than the one I had left. After many failed attempts at securing a decently clean and safe apartment—one potential landlord leered and said that I was welcome to have "men" visit me—I learned that my close friend Dana had unearthed an upcoming vacancy in her building. Dana is a child of Hungarian Holocaust survivors and she herself found an apartment in that building through her aunt, also a Holocaust survivor, who lived a couple of floors above her. The apartment was near Eglinton and Bathurst, a predominantly Jewish neighbourhood, and most of the tenants in the building were Jewish. I was granted an interview with the owner, during which I confessed I had a cat (actually I had two, but I only owned up to one). Oh no, he said, no pets are permitted. To my astonishment and shame—public display of emotion and special pleading go against my grain—I burst into tears. I've lost everything, I said, I can't lose my cat too. That good and kind man relented, accepting both me and my cat. If only I could tell him now what that gesture meant to me.

And so for two years I lived down the hall from my dear friend Dana and I wish I had been a better friend to her, but she had just had her first baby and was completely and un-selfconsciously wrapped up in new motherhood. I could not take pleasure in her pleasure. Visiting in her apartment, going to the park, simply being in the presence of a baby... these activities were unbearably painful for me. During those years I felt like my skin had been stripped away and the underlying tissue exposed to the elements.

But I did get down to work. I got a small grant from the teachers' union at York that, with a lot of financial scrimping, enabled me to take time off from teaching to finish my dissertation. I secured a carrel in the basement of the Robarts Library at the University of Toronto and every weekday I would get dressed, take the bus to the subway, the subway to the St. George station, and then walk the few blocks to the library. This was before the age of the laptop, and I would handwrite the pages of my dissertation during the day and type them up each night at home.

The Robarts Library, which opened in the early 1970s, was built in the brutalist tradition, all concrete and sharply jutting angles. Rumour had it that the long, zigzagging, concrete main entryway was designed to foil student protests and occupations of the building. When I worked there in the early mid-1980s the library still had an oddly retro-futuristic pneumatic tube system in place for ordering library books. You filled out the little form, tucked it into a cylinder, and it was magically sucked out of your hand and sent... who knows where. There were lovely carrels throughout the fourteen floors of the library, all of them reserved for University of Toronto students and professors. The ones in the basement were available to York University graduate students. They were about the size of two toilet cubicles stuck together and, as with toilet cubicles, the walls and doors were open at the top and bottom, so that you could hear all the coughs and sneezes and whispered conversations in the room. There was a desk in each carrel and we could keep our checked-out library books there. I hadn't been working in my carrel very long before I realized that the carrel next door to mine belonged to Jacqui. I think she only appeared once, and very briefly, to work in that space. When no one was looking, I peeped through the crack in the door and saw that her carrel was elaborately decorated, posters and postcards and other bits of colourful ephemera, all evidence of a large and confident personality, happy to claim her space.

At noon I would leave the library and walk around the neighbourhood, periodically checking in at the Toronto Women's Bookstore on Harbord Street and the Bob Miller Book Room on Bloor. Sometimes I would walk west along Bloor, in the opposite direction from the tony Yorkville shops, past the numerous Hungarian restaurants toward Honest Ed's emporium at the corner of Bloor and Bathurst. Scattered among the small ethnic restaurants in that area of Bloor Street were a bare handful of cool, alternative cafés and eateries, among them Chicken Licken. The restaurant was on a street corner and happy cartoon chickens strutted across its large plate glass windows. It was, in fact, a vegetarian restaurant that had taken over the space from Chicken Licken and—in an ironic, postmodern gesture—left the name and garish chickens in place. There was a sign in the window by the door that read: "We have no chicken today." In warm weather the door was propped open, and as I walked by, classical music, probably CBC FM radio, wafted out. The restaurant looked very hip. Very hip people sat at the tables. The food was probably delicious. But I never went in. Instead I retraced my steps along Bloor Street to the McDonald's where I ordered a McChicken burger and a small black coffee. I sat at a table on the second floor and eavesdropped on the conversations around me before I headed back to work.

I love hip restaurants and I see myself as the kind of person who frequents them. So why didn't I eat at Chicken Licken? This question returned to me a quarter of a century later when I was having lunch with a former PhD student, now a good friend, at a very hip restaurant in Edmonton. Jacqui came in alone, sat comfortably at a table, and ordered a full hot meal, probably her main meal of the day. The staff there knew her and she confidently, happily, and chattily occupied her space and enjoyed her food. What stopped me from dining alone at a hip restaurant, but not a McDonald's, back in the early mid-1980s when I was trying to recover a sense of myself, trying to be the person I had once imagined myself to be?

Newly separated from my husband, I moved into my apartment. I painted it a warm shade of grey, bought industrial shelves for my books and perforated paper up-and-down blinds that let in traceries of light. I bought a queen-sized futon bed. I exercised in the living room to Bruce Springsteen's *Born in the USA*.

And mostly I felt invisible. No longer a wife, never to be a mother, a young bourgeois-by-default woman who had accommodated the ambitions of a man who promised to do the same for her, but didn't. In the street I was often mistaken for being in the same ethnic group as whoever approached me. "You're a Jewish girl, aren't you?" said one grateful old woman when I saved her arthritic legs by going into the convenience store to buy her bus tickets. Women opened conversations with me at streetcar stops in their native Italian or Portuguese.

Was there a me there? I guess it turned out that there was, though it might not have been the me I once aspired to. But there was enough of that girl and woman to go alone all the way across the country to a new city, where she knew no one, and build a new life there, to challenge herself at work, to make new friends, and to share more than thirty years with a genuinely good man. And, in the end, to reach out to old friends and sometime rivals, connecting across a newly shared sense of mortality.

# Mars

I AM SURPRISED TO DISCOVER IN MYSELF A DEEP yearning to go to Mars, our little sister planet. I want to stand on its red, brown, gold, and tan surface, scan its horizon, and gaze at its two potato-shaped moons. This all started with NASA's Perseverance rover whose adventures I follow on Instagram. Perseverance is the fifth rover sent to Mars by NASA, the first being Sojourner in 1997. Sojourner's mission was expected to last only seven sols, though, in the end, it continued to send information back to Earth for eighty-three sols or eight-five Earth days. Subsequent rovers have also proven to have unexpectedly lengthy life spans, anywhere from six to twelve Earth years. Who knows how long Perseverance will continue to send back photographs and videos? Who knows how long it will continue to drill little bits of Martian rock as it goes about its mission to "Seek signs of ancient life and collect samples of rock and regolith (broken rock and soil) for possible return to Earth" (NASA).

The romance of Mars is captured in part by the idea of the "sol," a term for the Martian solar day. Wikipedia defines it as the "apparent interval between two successive returns of the Sun to the same meridian (sundial time) as seen by an observer on Mars." As seen by an observer on Mars! How I would love to be that observer and—because the Martian sol is twenty-four hours, thirty-nine minutes, thirty-five seconds long—to be just slightly out of whack with Earth time.

But, of course, the real attraction of Mars is its landscape, achingly familiar but also *unheimlich*, uncanny; *unheimlich* because familiar. The sun sets on Mars as it does on Earth, though the Martian dusk has a bluish tinge, not reddish as it does here. The Martian landscape includes rocks, deltas, old river beds, hills and mountains, a valley—the Valles Marineris—ten times the size of the Grand Canyon, and an enormous shield volcano—the Olympus Mons—two-and-a-half times higher than Mount Everest. Clouds sometimes drift over its summit. There is wind, and dust devils appear periodically on the surface of the planet. Mars has geologic periods, some marked by meteor impacts, another by volcanic activity and what NASA has described as "catastrophic flooding." But for what or whom would the flooding have been catastrophic? Freud's concept of the *unheimlich* or the uncanny suggests that "the uncanny is that class of the frightening which leads back to what is known of old and long familiar."

You see where I'm going with this. Curiosity Rover's 2019 discovery of large concentrations of methane gas suggests to some scientists, some astrobiologists, that DNA life may have begun elsewhere than on Earth. Did *we* begin elsewhere? Does Mars evoke some unbelievably primitive, primordial "experience of the human species"? In a 2019 *New Yorker* interview, biologist and genetics professor Gary Ruvkun suggests that "life didn't start here [on Earth]. It just landed here." It's possible, he says, that bacteria, which he describes as "incredibly complicated," "got here as soon as the Earth cooled, and they just started growing. And they've been spreading across the Milky Way and maybe the whole universe."

This whole idea is called *panspermia*, the notion that viable organisms are shared between planets and across star systems, often by meteorites. As an old hippy *manqué*, of course it makes me think of "Woodstock," the Crosby, Stills, Nash & Young tune, written by Joni Mitchell. The song suggests that humanity is composed of ancient stardust, cosmic carbon, and that we long to return to the "garden" of our origins. Maybe Mars, as its dry riverbeds suggest, was once such a garden.

Oh, man. How can these astrophysicists and astrobiologists and astronomers live with what they know and not go completely mad? The scope of things is JUST. SO. BIG. In a recent column, in the *London Review of Books*, about the new James Webb Telescope, professor of astrophysics Chris Lintott writes that observations from the earlier Hubble Telescope give us "a picture of a time when black holes were still assembling, and star formation was at its peak. The universe has been less exciting ever since." Less exciting! Now that Mars is within human reach and we have better pictures than ever of the giant gas planet Jupiter, all of this right in our own neighbourhood! And when Ruvkun can observe, really very casually, that the "Earth is 4.5 billion years old. And the universe, at least based on estimates from the Big Bang, is something like fourteen billion years."

But Professor Ruvkun, I cry, what was there before the universe? This was a question that plagued my childhood: What was before the universe? Can you get to the end of the universe? What is beyond it? I drove my mother crazy. What is at the end of the universe, or before the universe, is a metaphysical problem; for some it is a religious problem, but surely it is also a problem in basic logic. Ray Bradbury's 1950 collection, *The Martian Chronicles*, opens with an invented epigraph: " 'It is good to renew one's wonder,' said the philosopher. 'Space travel has again made children of us all.'" The astro-scientists have managed to hold on to their profound childhood curiosity and to hold on to it fearlessly. I say fearlessly because the enormity of it all can be, well, kind of terrifying.

I felt this terrifying enormity in my very young adulthood. I dropped acid a couple of times when I was seventeen and my first "trip," to use the lingo, was not pleasant. It was late at night and I was sitting outside with friends, looking up at the sky. The trees, bending with the wind, looked like they were dealing decks of cards. Let me hasten to say that this was an impression, not a hallucination. In retrospect, I like to imagine that they were tarot cards, the trees dispassionately laying out our futures. Beyond the trees it seemed that the universe was slowly spinning in complete and cold indifference, and I felt that we were all individual planets, totally isolated and alone, spinning in the cold dark. This was the time of my first boyfriend, my first love, and he was threatening to kill himself. I'm sure that inflected the nature of my LSD experience and my feeling of terrible isolation. I got home in the small hours of the morning and my mother was sitting angrily in the kitchen, waiting up for me. I slipped past with a quick greeting—after all, I was still high on LSD—and went to my room.

Three or four years later, post-boyfriend, I am sitting on the front steps of my parents' house, a glass of port in my hand. It is a crystal old-fashioned or lowball glass and there are ice cubes in my port, a drink I fancied at the time. It must have been a summer of increased sunspot activity because there were unusually frequent displays of northern lights in the skies above Montreal. I lie on my back in the cool damp grass and watch them. The universe does not feel indifferent. It feels... calm, as if it is pleasantly unfolding to all its possibilities. I get up and pick up the glass of port which slips from my hand. The crystal shatters into tiny shards, the shards seeming to reflect the stars in the sky. My mother seethes a little in the background, angry that I am drinking port, angry that I broke the glass. But, of course, she says nothing.

It is surprising how recent is our sense of intimacy with Mars. When Ray Bradbury began writing his Martian stories in the very late 1940s, he imagined a Mars with thin but breathable air. A Mars inhabited by an advanced civilization many tens of thousands of years old, and yet a civilization completely unaware of the existence of Earth. The Martians receive some hint that their lives are about to change, the intimation arriving via Earth poetry and song. A Martian woman dreams of a tall Earth man who sings to her, woos her with Ben Jonson's "Drink to me only with thine eyes, and I will pledge with mine." A Martian opera singer is surprised and frightened when the song that leaves her lips is Byron's "She walks in beauty like the night." When the first Earth missions land on Mars they are surprised to be greeted with apparent indifference. The indifference of the native Martians is short-lived, if only because they very soon succumb to chickenpox, an obvious parallel to the decimation of indigenous populations in the Americas by diseases brought by the early explorers. And, of course, the Earth men do not bring poetry with them; they bring only an interest in extracting resources. One man, Benjamin Driscoll, sees himself as the Johnny Appleseed of Mars. He conducts what he thinks of as "a private horticultural war with Mars," determined to plant enough trees, Earth trees, to create a more oxygen-rich atmosphere on the planet and make it friendlier to human habitation. That now seems such an insensitive and misguided relationship to a beautiful and mysterious planet.

For most of my life, I've harboured a kind of fantasy that when you die, the mysteries of the universe become clear. It's not so much that the mysteries are revealed as that you just know. You just know what came before the universe and what lies beyond the universe. My extremely limited knowledge of Buddhism is and is not helpful here. One site tells me that "Those well-trained in meditation have a chance to fuse into the clear light of absolute reality, which shines soon after death." Does the clear light of absolute reality include answers to the nature of the universe? The well-respected Buddhist monk, the recently deceased Thich Nhat Hanh, says that "Our true nature is the nature of no birth and no death." "When conditions are sufficient things manifest. When conditions are no longer sufficient things withdraw." To my religiously and scientifically uneducated mind, this sounds a lot like the first law of thermodynamics: energy cannot be created nor destroyed.

And now my brain hurts, so let me withdraw in my own way with this observation. It is that, in recent years, I've also discovered in myself the less ambiguous hope—I call it hope but it's really more of a whimsy—that at death one's beloved dogs, long gone, are there to greet one, as if one had just walked in the door after running a few errands. I'm hardly alone in desiring this, but somehow the two fantasies—that the nature of the universe reveals itself, and that one's dogs are there—seem compatible. It is, after all, a friendly, homely universe.

# POSTSCRIPT

# Everything Wants to Live

God the engineer
the systems analyst
stays up late poring over
his spreadsheets
his flow charts,
labouring in his pool of light
the cool light of his desk lamp,
scheming to coax from out the morass
a faultless order.

His poet's heart began
with gravity,
the great yearning
conjuring stars from gas,
the moon pulling
oceans to her breast,
the dark earth saying
come home.

The planet, his favourite
thick with motion and volition
but uncreatured.

His gardener's heart then bent to tease
the first thin strand from fog,
strand upon strand upon strand
the fog became steam became life.
Filament and jelly and tendril
blood and bone and root.

The hard and hot and molten
yielding to polymer and protein.

Rock splits but life seeds.
The earth an opal, *upala* precious stone
its blue milk bearing legion.

Soon the very air
Is dense with buzzing,
the corn so thick the mice
are trapped between its stalks.
The forests groan
beneath the weight of birds.
The streams and rivers stiffen
with the slimy and the scaled,
their shoals shoved gasping to the shore.
Bison bruised in their hordes,
deer and moose tangled in their horns.
It's all too much.

God panics
and goes to work.
The ancient of days bends
to his compass and protractor
his algorithms.
The solution when it comes is
so efficient, so economical
so elegant in its simplicity that
God punches the air. Eureka.
The bacteria feed the algae
feed the fish
feed the osprey.

It's perfect, it's perfect
he thinks.
Nothing created, nothing destroyed.

Panicked twittering
and the hawk in the tree
wings bent and spread for balance
tears into feathered flesh
scorning only twiglike legs,
the brittle tarsus.
The doe folds beneath the cougar's weight
in calm slow motion
front legs straining to regain her stance.
The spider clings to its web.
The dandelion clings to the earth
begging to go to seed.

Everything wants to live
the loud and silent prayers of everything
beseeching, imploring, begging.

Frustrated now, unthanked
"There is no death" God shouts to everything.
"There is no death."

# Notes

### Preface

Stevenson, Robert Louis. *The Strange Case of Dr. Jekyll and Mr. Hyde.* Longmans, Green & Co., 1886.

Woolf, Virginia. *Mrs. Dalloway.* ed. Jo-Ann Wallace. Broadview Press, 2013.

### 43 Leslie Gault

Mantel, Hilary. *Giving Up the Ghost: A Memoir.* Picador, 2003.

### Two Books

Annan, Noel. "The Intellectual Aristocracy." In *Studies in Social History*, edited by J. H. Plumb, 256–83. New York: Longmans Green, 1955.

[Anon.?] [Rev. of Ferguson 1858.] *The Reader*, Volume 4 (1864), 796.

Ferguson, Robert. *English Surnames and Their Place in the Teutonic Family*, 1858. Cited in Lower, Mark Antony. *Patronymica Britannica: A Dictionary of the Family Names of the United Kingdom.* London: J. R. Smith, 1860. Public Domain.

Gibb, Camilla. *Sweetness in the Belly.* Anchor Canada, 2006

Gilbreth, Frank B., Jr. and Ernestine Gilbreth Carey. *Belles on Their Toes.* New York: Thomas Y. Crowell Company, 1950.

O'Brien, Andy. *Rocket Richard.* Toronto: The Ryerson Press, 1961.

Palmer, Abram Smythe. *Folk Etymology: A Dictionary of Verbal Corruptions, Etc.* London: G. Bell and Sons, 1882.

Travers, P. L. *Mary Poppins Comes Back.* ill. Mary Shepard. New York: Harcourt Brace and Company, 1935.

### The Halfway Tavern

Hemingway, Ernest. "A Good Café on the Place St-Michel" in *A Moveable Feast.* Scribner's, 1964.

Oveniran, Channon. "Rockhead's Paradise." *The Canadian*

*Encyclopedia*. Historica Canada. Last edited 1 November 2018. https://www.thecanadianencyclopedia.ca/en/article/rock-heads-paradise

## White Swan, Black Swan

Hilma af Klint's abstract painting was discovered to global acclaim in 2018, when the Guggenheim Museum mounted a major exhibit. Since then, a newly burgeoning field of scholarship on her, and on the other members of The Five, suggests that her work was much more collaborative than originally imagined. In particular, she may have worked especially closely with Anna Cassel.

Aberth, Susan L. "Spirited Away. Who Painted Hilma af Klint's Otherworldly Visions?" *Artforum*. 19 April 2023. https://www.artforum.com/columns/who-painted-hilma-af-klints-otherworldly-visions-252631/

Small, Zachary. "After the Sudden Heralding of Hilma af Klint, Questions and Court Fights." *New York Times*, 28 August 2023. https://www.nytimes.com/2023/08/28/arts/design/hilma-af-klint-legacy.html

Andersen, Hans Christian. "The White Swans" in *The Fairy Tales of Hans Christian Andersen*. Helen Stratton, ill. Edward E Hale, intro. J. P. Lippincott, 1899.

Jung, Carl G. "Approaching the Unconscious." In *Man and His Symbols*. ed. Carl G. Jung. Dell Publishing, 1968, 1975.

Taleb, Nassim Nicholas. *The Black Swan: The Impact of the Highly Improbable*. Random House, 2007.

## Caesar Salad

Kaufman, Philip, dir. *Invasion of the Body Snatchers*. United Artists. 1978.

Smith, Patti. *M Train*. Alfred A. Knopf, 2015.

## Mean Girls

Bendo, Daniella, Taryn Hepburn, Dale Spencer. "Compensating for Stigma: Representations of Hard-to-Adopt Children in 'Today's Child.'" *Journal of Childhood Studies* 46, 4 (December 2021): 1–16.

Waters, Mark, dir. *Mean Girls*. Broadway Video, Paramount Pictures. 2004.

## The Light Princess

MacDonald, George, *The Light Princess*. ill. Maurice Sendak. Farrar, Straus and Giroux, 1969.

## Elvira Madigan

Widerberg, Bo, dir. *Elvira Madigan*. Europa Film, 1967.

## The Mercenary

Seymour, Miranda. *In My Father's House: Elegy for an Obsessive Love*. Pocket Books, 2008. [First published Simon & Schuster UK Ltd., 2007.]

## Carole with an E

Lessing, Doris. *Martha Quest*. Panther Books Ltd., 1966 [rpt. 1975].

## Uncle Joe

Hefner, Hugh, host. "Playboy's Penthouse." Hugh Hefner to Lenny Bruce. Season One, Episode One, 1959.

## North American Factors

Investopedia, s.v. "Factor Definition: Requirements, Benefits, and Example." 31 March, 2022. https://www.investopedia.com/terms/f/factor.asp

Gray, Peter. "The Rise and Fall of Freedom in Education in the 1960s and '70s." *Psychology Today*, 22 January 2023. https://www.psychologytoday.com/ca/blog/freedom-to-learn/202301/

the-rise-and-fall-of-freedom-in-education-in-1960s-and-70s

Neill, A. S. *Summerhill: A Radicial Approach to Child Rearing.* Foreward, Erich Fromm. Hart Publishing Company, 1960.

Untermeyer, Louis. *A Concise Treasury of Great Poems.* Pocket Books, 1966.

**Whimsy**

Goffman, Erving. *Asylums: Essays on the Condition of the Social Situation of Mental Patients and Other Inmates.* Anchor Books, 1961.

Koster, Henry, dir. *Harvey.* Universal Pictures. 1951.

**Me and Not-Me**

Ernaux, Annie. *Happening.* Trans. Tanya Leslie. Seven Stories Press, 2019. Orig. pub. Éditions Gallimard, 2000.

Finch, Annie, ed. *Choice Words: Writers on Abortion.* Haymarket Books, 2020.

Zernike, Kate. "Is a Fetus a Person? An Anti-Abortion Strategy Says Yes." *New York Times.* Aug. 21, 2022; updated Aug. 30, 2022. https://www.nytimes.com/2022/08/21/us/abortion-anti-fetus-person.html

**Poetry**

*The Glass Bead Game* is the name of Herman Hesse's 1943 novel (also published under the title *Magister Ludi*). Centuries in the future, a province in central Europe is the preserve of an order of ascetic intellectuals who devote their lives to playing the arcane and abstract glass bead game.

Hesse, Herman. *The Glass Bead Game.* Holt, Rinehart and Winston, 1943; 1949 English edition.

Patchett, Ann. *Truth and Beauty: A Friendship.* HarperCollins, 2004.

"Time's wingèd chariot" is from Andrew Marvell's c. 1681 poem "To His Coy Mistress."

"This too too solid flesh" is from Hamlet's famous soliloquy in act I, scene 2 of Shakespeare's *Hamlet.*

"It is the blight man was born for" is from Gerard Manley Hopkins's 1880 (pub. 1918) poem "Spring and Fall: To a Young Child."

## Melmac

Maté, Gabor. *In the Realm of Hungry Ghosts: Close Encounters with Addiction.* Knopf Canada, 2008.

Wright, Russel and Mary Einstein Wright. *Guide to Easier Living.* Simon and Schuster, 1951.

## Virginia Woolf's Commas

Shields, E. F. "The American Edition of *Mrs. Dalloway.*" *Studies in Bibliography* 27 (1974): 157–75.

References to the "Unreal City" and "carbuncular clerks" are from T. S. Eliot's 1922 poem, "The Waste Land."

## I Don't Care About This Anymore

Biggs, Joanna. "The Earth Had Need of Me." *London Review of Books*, 16 April 2020, 7–12.

Woolf, Virginia. *To the Lighthouse.* Hogarth Press, 1927.

## The Penny Drops

Didion, Joan. "On Keeping a Notebook." *Slouching Towards Bethlehem.* Farrar, Straus and Giroux, 1968.

Levy, Deborah. *The Cost of Living: A Living Autobiography.* Hamish Hamilton, 2018.

## Iceland

Krasskova, Galina. *Living Runes: Theory and Practice of Norse Divination.* Weiser Books, 2010, 2019.

## Patina

Craig, Lawrence. "Metal Founders Since 1851." *Maclean's Magazine.* 1 March 1930: 19–21.

## The Women's Ward

Davies, Robertson. *Fifth Business*. Macmillan Canada, 1970.

## Mars

Bradbury, Ray. *The Martian Chronicles*. Avon Books, 1997 ed. Orig. pub. Doubleday, 1950.

Chotiner, Isaac. "What If Life Did Not Originate on Earth?" Interview with Gary Ruvkun. *The New Yorker*, 8 July 2019. https://www.newyorker.com/news/q-and-a/what-if-life-did-not-originate-on-earth.

Freud, Sigmund. "The Uncanny." *The Standard Edition of the Complete Psychological Works of Sigmund Freud*. Vol. XVII. Trans. and ed., James Strachey. The Hogarth Press, 1955.

Lintott, Chris. "Born in Light." *London Review of Books* 44, 2 (27 January 2022). https://www.lrb.co.uk/the-paper/v44/n02/chris-lintott/short-cuts

Holmes, Ken. "Buddhism and Death." https://www.samyeling.org/buddhism-and-meditation/teaching-archive-2/dharmacharya-ken-holmes/buddhism-and-death/

Thich Nhat Hanh. *No Death, No Fear*. Riverhead Books, New York, 2002.

# Acknowledgements

*These little pieces of my life* would not have been written if not for the women—the late Margaret-Ann Armour, Patricia Clements, Isobel Grundy, Margaret Mackey, Jeanne Perreault—who joined me, some years ago, in a little, Bloomsbury-inspired memoir club. I thank you all from the bottom of my heart for sharing your lives, in so many ways, with me.

Stephen Slemon has graciously listened to early drafts of almost every one of these pieces (they were originally written for the ear), and his editorial advice has been invaluable. Judy Kalman has read them as they came out and encouraged me every step of the way.

I couldn't have found my way to a better literary press. Working with Thistledown has been a gift. Elizabeth Philips, Acquisitions Editor, is a model of clear and transparent communication. Rilla Friesen, Managing Editor, guided me patiently through filling out online forms. Betsy Rosenwald designed the cover of my dreams, and kindly brought my attention to the latest research on artist Hilma af Klint. Thistledown recommended that I work with Susan Olding as my editor. I couldn't be more grateful. She was enthusiastic, encouraging, and most importantly, spot on in her recommendations for improvement.

How can I fully acknowledge everything that Stephen Slemon has been to this project and to me? I can't. So I'll simply thank him and Allie Slemon for being such big pieces in my small life.

# Journal Acknowledgements

A handful of these pieces have been published, sometimes in a somewhat different form, in the following journals. "Virginia Woolf's Commas" appeared as "On Typing" in the *London Review of Books* (24 February 2022). "Cancer in the Time of Covid" appeared as "Cancer during COVID-19 freed me to drop the 'bucket list' and just live" in the Toronto *Globe and Mail* (23 September 2022). "Patina" appeared in the *Literary Review of Canada* (July/August 2022). "Melmac" appeared as "The Melmac Years" in the *Literary Review of Canada* (September 2023). "Elvira Madigan" appeared in *Prairie Schooner* (Summer 2023).

Photo: Stephen Slemon

JO-ANN WALLACE was an Emeritus Professor in the Department of English and Film Studies at the University of Alberta. In her younger years, her poetry appeared in several now defunct periodicals, including *The Canadian Forum*. Her scholarly work focused on little known progressive movements and women writers of the late nineteenth and early twentieth centuries. More recently, her literary nonfiction appeared in venues like the *London Review of Books*, the *Literary Review of Canada*, and *Prairie Schooner*. At the time of her death in June 2024, she was living in Victoria with her husband Stephen Slemon and their rambunctious dog Bodhi.